FIVE-STAR CUSTOMER SERVICE

TED COINÉ

FIVE-STAR CUSTOMER SERVICE

iUniverse books may be ordered through booksellers or by contacting:

iUniverse
1663 Liberty Drive
Bloomington, IN 47403
www.iuniverse.com
844-349-9409

ISBN: 978-1-6632-4029-3 (sc)
ISBN: 978-1-6632-4030-9 (e)

Print information available on the last page.

iUniverse rev. date: 06/01/2022

To Jane,

my personal customer service guru

Foreword

"Your challenge is not just to improve.
It is to break the service paradigm
in your industry or market
so that customers aren't just satisfied,
they're so shocked that they tell strangers
on the street how good you are."
- Jack Welch, *Winning*

I read business books all the time – I try to average two per month – and I always ask the same question before I pick my next read: What makes this author an expert?

If I were you, that's exactly what I'd be saying right now: Who is this Ted Coiné character, and what qualifies him as an expert in five-star customer service?

Let me answer this question for you, in reverse chronological order. We'll start with what I do for a living: in the process of teaching any type of course, I train companies in five-star customer service, as do my colleagues at Coiné Corporate Training. These companies pay us well to do it. They're always happy with their results; I've been told that we don't charge enough. That to me is all of the qualification we need.

But maybe not to you, so here's some more. My company also consistently *provides* five-star customer service. I'll share some of our practices in the chapters that follow, so you can judge for yourself. But I make this claim only after years of feedback from numerous clients, strategic partners, and students. We continually surprise these people with how helpful we are, and with how dramatically we exceed their already high expectations. Like George Boldt (Chapter 1), we don't really see this as anything but business as usual; I'm sometimes surprised when I receive a compliment from a client. What did they expect, I wonder? And is everyone else they work with so bad?

The reason for this book, in fact, is that the answer to that last question is a resounding "Yes!" Even in our customer-service obsessed culture, ninety percent of the companies out there provide sub-par service, and the next nine percent still have plenty of room for improvement. What we teach is desperately needed.

We started our efforts not by teaching customer service per se, but rather as an integral part of our English as a Second Language (ESL) courses. You see, we customize all of our courses so that we can teach the corporate culture and practices of each company with whom we work. When that company is dedicated to outstanding customer service, as are Lifeline Systems, Roche Bros. Supermarkets, and Legal Sea Foods (to name just a few), the material we develop for their ESL course rubs off on us. And, better yet for all concerned, the lessons we pick up from one employer are usually applicable to the others. Naturally, we would never train competitors in each other's practices, but when the fields are as different as the three I mentioned above ...hey, why not?

To take it one step further, we found early on that the things we were training our ESL students to do so impressed their managers, they started teaching our material to their American employees! It's an honor when you find you're actually teaching new customer service practices to an organization already widely recognized as four- or five-star.

Going back further still, I owe much of what's made me an expert in this field to my wife, Jane. She started working as a customer service manager for Roche Bros. when she was twenty-two. For sixteen years, all she did was work for that top-notch customer service firm, and she was a company star, until she stepped down to help me as C.O.O. of our own company. Now she's our star.

The stories Jane told me about Roche Bros.' customer service standards used to floor me. I remarked more than once that they were crazy, as when she told me about giving a new roast beef to a lady who'd clearly overcooked her last one. The customer claimed the cut of meat (and not her cooking) was to blame, so she wanted them to do something about it – and they replaced it, without hesitation! How could they run a company that way? I marveled.

But after a while, this and other stories didn't seem so strange. Now they seem ...well... normal.

I now realize I've been learning the values of customer service all my life. In my sales career, I had to build and maintain relationships with a number of demanding multi-millionaires, many of whom viewed extraordinary customer service almost as their birthright. In college and directly after, I earned my way as a waiter and bartender at some fancy (as well as a few seedy) nightspots. By providing superior customer service, I thrived in that profession. I learned at the feet of my parents, both exacting professionals whose impossibly high standards I've struggled my whole life to meet. The manners they drilled into me as a child were an essential part of my customer service training. Even when I was three I had already started learning the all-important Customer Service Ethic that is the foundation of our firm's entire training regimen. To find out more on that one, you'll have to read the section about Stew Leonard's.

Ultimately, I think the question of my qualifications will come down to one issue: Can I teach what you need to know? To that question, only you have the answer. All I can say is, if you read this entire book cover to cover and don't garner any new lessons from it, I want to hear from you, so I can learn *your* secrets! Even the best teacher has more to learn.

Some Notes Before We Begin

The purpose of this book is to teach the Customer Service Ethic, as it is explained in Chapter 1. The contents will be helpful to every level of customer service provider. However, it is geared toward customer service professionals who are now providing two-, three-, and even four-star customer service at present.

This book is intended to bring five-star values and performance to organizations that are *not* exclusive, that *don't* cater to the richest and most exacting 1%. Ideally, it will help people working for average, every-day companies to learn and, with practice, to master the outstanding customer service that is typically reserved for the rich and famous.

This is a selfish dream of mine, actually. You see, nothing would make me happier than to walk into my local bank, pharmacy, or convenience store and get the kind of service I describe in the pages that follow. Just the thought of calling my town hall at lunch hour and reaching a cheery, helpful, *live* person is almost more than I can imagine.

Even if you are currently providing five-star customer service, I'll bet you'll find some things in this book that you don't already know or do.

…And if you're reading this book, there's actually a good chance that you're already at a four- or five-star level. Polished professionals are so good because they're always working to better themselves, even once they've reached the top. To put my own twist on a hackneyed expression, superlative customer service isn't a destination; it's an everyday practice. Sit on your laurels, or on the reputation of your organization, and you'll soon be in big trouble.

I do not promise that you will master five-star service after completing this book. That really depends on you: on where you are now, and how well you take these lessons to heart. Still, even if you don't reach the top right away, this will give you a terrific head start in your journey toward excellence.

Sprinkled throughout the text are discussion questions. You should pause to answer them before going on. It will reinforce what you're learning and give you some unexpected new insights into your own beliefs, practices, and goals.

I strongly recommend you keep a logbook in addition to this book. Record your own customer service experiences, both as a private citizen and as a budding customer service expert. Even collect your friends' stories. This will dramatically speed your growth as a five-star customer service provider. Remember, the more you practice and reflect and practice and teach, the faster you'll develop.

Contents

1

THE CUSTOMER SERVICE ETHIC

"A job well done is its own reward."
- Benjamin Franklin

What is the Customer Service Ethic?

If asked to define customer service, I'm sure that most of us could easily think of an example or ten of good or bad service just from our experiences in the past week: a check-out clerk who said, "Have a nice day" and actually meant it; a doctor's receptionist who squeezed you in for a last-minute visit; a waiter who recommended against the most expensive item on the menu, tip-be-damned….

Usually, the situations that come to mind, positive or negative, involve the service industry in some way – which, of course, is how that industry got its name in the first place.

But what about that doctor's receptionist? Surely, she's not a waiter, store clerk, or hotel worker. How did she make the list?

And if a receptionist can be included in the field of customer service, who else belongs there?

The fact of the matter is that five-star customer service is not exclusive to elite hotels, resorts, and restaurants. Surely, you'll run into it aplenty at such places. It'll be obscenely expensive, the kind of thing only one or two percent of the population could even hope to afford. But the good news is, you'll also bump into it in the unlikeliest of places: at the El Cheapo gas station down the street, from your ten-year-old paperboy; from your garbage man, when he holds up his route so you can run out with your barrels early one day, then places them down gently so as not to destroy your flower garden.

Yes, anyone can provide five-star customer service. So you can, too. All you have to do is master the Customer Service Ethic described in this first chapter, learn a few basic practices, and you'll be on your way.

Discussion Questions

1. In the space below, list at least ten jobs in which the workers engage in customer service. Try to challenge yourself, thinking beyond the obvious, traditional service-industry fields.

2. As your list grows, see if you can form a general rule as to what kind of jobs involve customer service.

3. What ties them all together?

STOP!!! Do not turn the page until you have answered these questions.

We are ALL in
customer service.

Surprised? Disagree? That's understandable. After all, how does a research scientist engage in customer service? Who are her customers? How is operating a forklift a service function? What in the role of computer programmer involves human interaction at all, not to mention customer service? And certainly, the role of "Boss" (manager, vice president; company owner) has nothing to do with customers *or* service – it has to do with giving orders, and receiving service from your minions! Right?

Wrong, wrong, and …quite wrong. The fact is, any time we interact with others in any capacity, we have the opportunity to wow them with our Customer Service Ethic or chill them with our poor service. When we work alone? A job well done provides good customer service. Work done in a shoddy manner, or that does not provide what is requested, or is delivered late or over budget, means that you are providing bad customer service – which is actually customer *dis*service, when you think about it.

Which brings us back to our first question. What is the Customer Service Ethic?

We're not talking about right and wrong, good and bad in this context. You're not going to go to jail for failing to smile when you greet a customer, though the rest of us sometimes wish that you would.

Rather, another word for *ethic* in this sense is *value*, as in your personal values: what you hold most dear in defining yourself as a person. The Customer Service Ethic is a core belief that all customer service professionals treasure. And because it is a central value, this ethic dictates all that we do. For the true customer service professional, to be accused of delivering inadequate customer service is to be found lacking in a fundamental way. We will take great pains not to get stuck with such a label.

Discussion Question

1.   Take a few minutes to develop a working definition of what lies at the heart of the Customer Service Ethic. It can be one word, a list of words, or even a sentence. You can write your definition in the space below.

STOP!!! Do not turn the page until you are finished with this exercise.

Pride

Pride. That's my definition of the Customer service Ethic. Just one word, a succinct explanation that I find sums up the entire philosophy behind five-star customer service.

How does my answer compare to yours? Remember, this is philosophy and social science, not engineering. That means your answer, though phrased differently, may jibe perfectly with mine. Yours might even be better.

But what does this word really mean? And, much more importantly for you, how is it translated into everyday habits and practices that together allow you, the customer service professional, to deliver the five-star customer service that is going to transform your company and your career?

The answer to *that* question is what the entire remainder of this book, and our training courses, is all about.

But first things first. You're not going to master any skill until you completely grasp and then "own" the principle that governs it. Personal and professional pride, which we call the Customer Service Ethic, is the foundation to the castle you will build, which we call five-star customer service.

It's time for a story to illustrate how the Customer Service Ethic works and, when working well, how it can transform a life.

George Boldt,
The Greatest Customer Service
Professional of Them All

America was a different place in 1892. There was no income tax. You could live like a king on a few thousand dollars a year. Certainly you could build a beautiful, spacious home for under one thousand dollars. Meanwhile, a handful of industrialists, the Robber Barons, were amassing fortunes of hundreds of millions of dollars.

William Waldorf Astor was the heir of the first Robber Baron, and in 1892, even with giants like Rockefeller and Carnegie in the mix, he was still one of the richest men on earth – richer even than the Queen of England.

But even he needed a place to sleep each night, and one night in 1892 he found himself on business in Philadelphia without a hotel reservation.

Enter George Boldt. A German immigrant, Boldt had done well for himself. By 1892 he was the general manager of Philadelphia's most exclusive hotel, the Bellevue-Stratford. Every one of his guests was wealthy and important, and his hotel flourished because he treated them accordingly.

Then one night a guest arrived. In these days before mass media, even the country's most famous citizens went through much of their lives anonymously. So when Astor arrived at Bellevue's front desk that night, all Boldt knew was that he was a man in need of a room.

Boldt met the man and introduced himself as the hotel manager. Astor did not say his own name. He merely repeated his request for a room.

"Sir," Boldt said, "I'm afraid all of the rooms in our hotel are full. However, it would be my pleasure to have the housekeeping staff prepare my family rooms for you. You can stay as my guest; my family and I will lodge with the staff tonight. Please give me thirty minutes to make the arrangements."

Little did he know it when he made the offer, but George Boldt's life was about to change dramatically. For Astor was impressed. So impressed that the next morning, after a good night's sleep and a sumptuous breakfast in Boldt's apartment, Astor made an offer of his own to George Boldt.

"Mr. Boldt," Astor said. "I am currently in the process of building a hotel in Manhattan, and it is my intention to make it the world's greatest. It is clear to me after all you have done that you must be the manager of my hotel; in fact, no one else will do. Kindly name your price, and the job is yours."

Boldt was happy at his hotel in Philadelphia; it was a good job, and his family had deep roots there. He didn't need Astor's offer. But by now he knew who Astor was, and he already knew all about Astor's reputation as a shrewd businessman. Boldt asked for the moon. Why not, he thought? He had nothing to lose if Astor turned him down.

"My price is one million dollars a year," Boldt said. Remember, this was before the income tax. Indeed, with inflation, the amount translates into closer to a billion dollars in today's world. George Boldt fully expected Astor to laugh in his face.

Astor didn't laugh at all. He didn't even hesitate, phenomenal as the sum was.

"Mr. Boldt," Astor replied, "That is an astronomical amount of money. But, had you asked for more, I would have paid it. You are worth every penny."

As you might imagine, Boldt's life was transformed. Astor's hotel, the Waldorf-Astoria, remains to this day the most famous, prestigious – and probably expensive! – hotel in the world. Boldt ended up owning the hotel. He built a castle on the water in New York's Thousand Islands, which today is a national park. His great-grandchildren, whom I happen to know as stepsiblings, all have trust funds. They also share some amazing family lore.

In a sense, Boldt won the lottery. As the slogan goes, "You can't win if you don't play." Now, no one's going to promise you a million dollars a year for becoming a five-star customer service professional. But of course, you never know what might happen if you impress the right customer....

Discussion Question

1. What lessons can be learned from George Boldt's story? How does the philosophy of the Customer Service Ethic, and its definition of Pride, relate to Boldt's experience? Try to list a few important points to be learned from all of this.

What do I, as a customer service professional, get out of the George Boldt story? To me, it's a story of how the Customer Service Ethic is meant to work.

The Customer Service Ethic is all about pride, and that's what drove George Boldt to do what he did when he offered his quarters to an unnamed guest.

The pride that Boldt felt was based on his self-image as a man who simply could never bring himself to say no to a customer. His choice that night was to let that man walk out of his hotel disappointed, or ...come up with a creative solution that allowed him to accommodate one more guest.

Now, that may seem like a choice to you and me; giving up your lush apartment for a dreary maid's room might not be your first choice, or even your last. *But to George Boldt, there was no choice to be made at all!* He had a room, he had a guest in need, and he had his pride as an hotelier who would never, *could* never, turn a would-be guest away.

George Boldt delivered five-star customer service that night in 1892, just as he did every day of his life. It made him immensely rich, and somewhat famous as well. It brought him the respect that few people in life deserve. Simply put, he did what he did better than anyone else, and he acted the way he did because that matched his self-image: he was a professional, and that's how professionals behave.

All right, enough about George Boldt. After all, he's been dead for most of a century. What does the whole issue of professional and personal pride have to do with you?

Remember, pride is what lies at the heart of the Customer Service Ethic. Pride is going to inspire you to act in ways that may at times be inconvenient. Excellent customer service is often all about making the tough choice; staying at work late to make sure a project gets done on time, arguing with a coworker to make a delivery happen properly, persuading your obstinate boss that she'll lose an important client if she doesn't do what you suggest; cleaning your company's public rest room yourself because it's disgusting, and the maintenance staff is not on hand, and after all, it's your company, too....

Once you truly "get it," you're going to find that your choices in certain matters are limited. Strange as it may sound, it's no longer your prerogative to come to work in anything but a good mood. You can't make yourself walk by litter outside your company's entrance anymore. When you've been baited by an absolutely miserable – even slightly abusive – irate customer, you will be reluctant to defend yourself – instead you'll say, "I'm sorry" …again!

But your job will hold different rewards, too. For one thing, your customers will be more pleasant, at least on average. Some will even ask for you by name, because you have helped them so well in the past. Your boss will compliment you more, and your review will reflect her new appreciation of you. You'll earn the admiration of your coworkers. They'll ask you for advice on how to do their own jobs better, they'll listen a bit more respectfully when you speak; now and then you'll even catch them talking about you when they think you're not around – but don't worry, it'll be in a good way. Do it right, and you'll be on the fast track for promotion.

Best of all? You'll feel better about yourself. "A job well done is its own reward," as Ben Franklin (America's first customer service trainer) wrote in *Poor Richard's Almanac*. The personal and professional pride that motivates you to go the extra mile in your customer service tasks will also leave you feeling …proud. And what could be better motivation than that?

From The Trenches

My Own (very modest) Boldt/Astor Story

As a waiter in college, I was certainly no George Boldt; nor were any of my patrons Astors. However, I did strive to give the best service I could, and in a few instances it paid off with more than just a generous tip.

On one such occasion, I waited on two customers who were clearly on a first date. The guy, "Big" Jim, was a few years out of college. His date, Leslie, was a sophomore I'd met through friends of friends one time. So I didn't actually know them, but that didn't matter: I gave them the same service I gave everyone else. I was friendly, like the unobtrusive host of a party. I suggested a new drink concoction that previous guests had been raving about, and it went over well. I laughed (sincerely) at a few of his jokes. Mostly all I did was stay out of their way.

Well, perhaps in some small part to me (though probably more to their own chemistry), the date was a success. And even though I thought nothing of the service I'd given, it made a bigger impression on Big Jim. In fact, he was so impressed with my style, and with my "obvious knowledge" of the bar, that he returned to my restaurant about two months later and offered me a job – as his bar manager.

I gladly took the job, and of course I tried to make him just as happy with his choice as possible. I knew nothing about bartending aside from the general concept that I could afford beer and little else. But I learned quickly, so this happy tale has a happy ending.

A waiter recruited to bartend. Whoop-de-do. But here's the thing: it *was* good for me; *very* good. I doubt it was much more than a lateral move at the time, and I had no ambitions to stay in the service industry after college. But life takes its own course sometimes, and on several occasions before I began teaching I used my bartending credentials as a fallback position when this or that career had stalled and I wasn't sure what was next. I also used my bartending resume to land jobs in several new cities after school, so I got to travel. Plus, bartending is a superb way to meet potential dates.

So what if I had given Big Jim average service? What if I'd been modestly efficient, but not all that jovial, and not at all proactive with my drink recommendations? And what if Leslie had hated Big Jim? What then?

Did providing excellent service get me a million-dollar-a-year salary, as it did George Boldt? No. But it made me feel good. It made my customers feel good as well. It helped me get a slightly better job, where the boss recruited *me* – something to pump up the ego a little, if nothing else. And it taught me an invaluable lesson about the power of customer service. Now *that* was a worthwhile experience.

Discussion Questions

1. What would happen if one of your customers were to open a business of his own, and had a job to fill that was a step or two up from your current position? Would he recruit you?

2. If your answer is No, what could you do differently in the present performance of your job that would change that answer?

Don't take these two questions lightly. My father's job for thirty years was to poach talent from one company to fill top spots in others. My own firm lost one of its best teachers to a recruiter who had the one thing we couldn't offer: a job right in her own town. George Boldt wasn't the only one to get "shopped" by an employer while at his work. Are you the type a recruiter would snap up, or the type that gets passed by?

2

WHAT IS FIVE-STAR
CUSTOMER SERVICE?

"Now what's your problem?"
- Anonymous donut shop clerk

What is the difference between four- and five-star service? I hear this question quite a bit in my line of work. Great service is great service, isn't it?

It's an excellent question. So let's take a chapter to discuss all of the stars, with plenty of examples to help you get a handle on exactly what each entails.

<u>Ted's Quick Guide to the Stars</u>:

No-Star: This rarity is reserved for when service is just plain insulting.

One-Star: This service is terrible. You're thoroughly displeased.

Two-Star: Mediocre. Nothing to be proud of at all.

Three-Star: Fine. No complaints. Also, not impressive in the least.

Four-Star: Outstanding. You are treated like a long-time customer even the first time they meet you.

Five-Star: Above any possible expectation – except perhaps if you're a multi-millionaire. "Service Extras" are standard and many.

Now, let's go into some detail.

No-Star "Service"

If customer service is nonexistent (pay-at-the-pump, for instance) or really, really bad, that's not no-star customer service. No-star service means you think the service provider belongs in jail, and his mother does as well.

A ready example is when a cabbie asks where you're going before he'll unlock the door to let you in. (Yes, that's illegal).

One time, a visit to New York City brought us to a tiny pizza joint. It was a few years ago, but I still remember looking around for the candid camera, because the counter clerk was so outrageously rude that it was almost funny. Among other offenses, he laughed contemptuously when I asked if they had something like Hawaiian pizza. Sadly, we were so starved that we paid for this abuse (and pepperoni slices) anyway.

Call me old fashioned, but I don't think you should openly scorn your customers.

Discussion Questions

1.   Can you recall a time when you received no-star customer service? Remember, it has to be *really* outrageous to qualify for this ignominy.

2.   Have you ever given no-star service? (Come on, be honest! We've all had bad days, bad work situations…)

This one doesn't take much thought. Atrocious service is atrocious service. Enough said.

One-Star Disservice

If this is the kind of service you currently provide and it doesn't embarrass you, kindly put this book down now. I can't help you.

If it *does* embarrass you, so much so that you want to change your evil ways… well then, we've got a lot of work ahead of us.

If you're on the customer end of this kind of service and if you're smart, you'll never return. Unless, that is, you're dealing with a monopoly, in which case you have no choice. The government (town, state, and federal) is a perfect example of how a one-star service provider can remain in business. Where else are you going to go for a driver's license?

One-star service is by definition frustrating. It is also often tacky. Let me illustrate.

Jane and I were at a bar in Newport, Rhode Island. This spunky little promotions girl came around asking if we'd like a shot of some trendy new liquor. As our motto is, "Who are we to say no?" we took her up on it. Then she said, "Want me to do one with you?" Sure, we said. Why not?

I'll tell you why not: as soon as our shots were downed, she said, "That's three shots. $18, please." It's the kind of thing my more traveled friends have told me about from their sojourns to third-world cantinas. Not exactly the kind of service you'd hope for in a swanky town such as Newport.

It wasn't no-star service. The girl was very pleasant; we weren't insulted or anything. It was certainly legal, but a bit dishonest, and left us feeling rather used. One-star all the way.

This is something you have to look out for in tourist towns, by the way. We've noticed this again and again on our travels.

Take Newport again: some of the best food we've ever eaten is served in that little resort town. But the service? Four- and five-star fare, delivered with three- or even two-star customer service, pretty much across the board.

Why are vacation destinations usually so lax in service? My belief is that it has to do with the nature of their business. Resorts don't typically get repeat customers, and certainly not regulars. Plus, you're a captive audience: where are you going to eat while on vacation to some remote island, if not on that island?

Poor service often thrives in situations where there are no good-service options available to the consumer. Again and again in this book, we'll discuss whole markets or entire industries in which you simply cannot find a good-service option. Among many others, these include banking, cellular service companies, medicine, the government, monopolies such as public utilities, and low-cost retail. In this type of environment, the consumer has no choice but to frequent poor-service providers.

It's my theory that if one organization in a given market begins to outshine its competitors in the customer service it provides, it will steal a huge chunk of market share, and so the investment it has made in its customer service training will be worth every penny. I know of too many successful companies that have built their reputations – and their fortunes – on vastly superior customer service to doubt this in the least. Poor customer service is penny-wise, but pound-foolish, no matter the field in question.

Discussion Questions

1. Is there any aspect of customer service at your company that can be described as one-star? Remember, while you may lie to yourself, your customers aren't going to be so kind.

2. Think of a situation where you received one-star customer service. How did it make you feel? Who did you tell? Did you patronize that business again?

3. How do institutions that provide one-star customer service stay in business? If they do remain in business, how do you think they do it?

4. Do you buy the "penny-wise, pound-foolish" argument I put forth at the end of this passage? Why or why not? Choose a field that you've noticed provides consistently bad service. What do you think would happen if one "player" in that field cleaned up its act and began to provide five-star customer service? Would it thrive, or perish? Would the money spent on customer service training be an expense (bad), or an investment (good)?

Standards of one-star service include:

- You feel unwelcome, perhaps even as if your presence is an interruption.
- Your experience is frustrating and dissatisfying.
- You want to write a letter of complaint to whoever is in charge.*
- You promise yourself you'll never go back.
- You pledge you'll tell all of your friends, so they'll stay away, too.
- Good luck getting a smile. Even simple eye contact is rare.
- Complaints are not redressed.
- There is no customer service number to call. Or there is, but you have to pay for trouble shooting by the minute.
- When you call, the phone just rings and rings. There is not even a machine to take your message.
- If the phone does pick up, there is no option of reaching a person, no matter what you try.
- All hospital emergency rooms provide one-star service.
- One-star example: The doctor's next appointment is six months out. In Massachusetts, at least, this describes every single dermatologist.
- One-star example: When you pick your car up from the garage, the problem you brought it in for may be

fixed. However, within a week you notice your brakes need fixing. Nobody bothered to tell you, so now you have to lose use of your car for a second time.

*Sadly for the upper management of one-star businesses, the urge to write a letter usually passes, and these folks have no idea how poorly their business is being run by the rank and file. Irate customers rarely write letters, email, or even call. They do tell their friends, however. Boy, do they tell their friends! So these businesses get hit by a double-whammy: no one is telling them what they're doing wrong, but everyone is telling his friends.

I used to write letters to the owner if I was truly offended by poor service. Then I had a change of heart: if the business owner allows service to be so bad that it angers me, why should I help him? If he means well, and simply has no idea that things on the front lines are all that bad, he's not much of a manager. The consumer's job is not to teach him his business. Now, I save myself the effort of a letter, and take my business elsewhere instead.

Two-Star Service

Two-star service is substandard; it's upsetting to all but the most abuse-resistant customers.

Sadly, it's quite common. Often providers of this type of service survive by attracting customers with low prices.

This cheap price/poor service/cheap quality formula is actually built into their business model. There are companies that thrive on this, as a matter of fact. And hey, if you're not expecting much and don't get much, how can you be disappointed?

Before you judge too harshly, think about Dunkin Donuts and Starbucks. Now, Starbucks is hoity-toity and gourmet, but it's also expensive. In most respects it's a four-star joint – although we'll have to return to its customer service a little later.

Dunkin Donuts coffee is pretty good (rather than gourmet). The atmosphere of its stores is more blue-collar, and the prices are somewhat more reasonable. It has a two-star image. I expect two-star service from Dunkin, and am rarely disappointed or surprised. So you see, two-star service has its place.

But its place is not in this book. Two-star service may pay the bills, but it doesn't make anyone proud.

Standards of two-star service include:

- Turnover is such that you see a new clerk every time you patronize the business. As a result, you are always treated like a first-time customer.
- It's hard to get a smile, even if you try to coax one out.

- The staff's idea of conversation with the customer is to complain about their day, the last customer, the company, etc.

- Staff members chat amongst themselves to the detriment of attentive service.

- You have to wait. A lot.

- Giving an apology is not even conceivable to the staff.

- You've either never seen a manager, or the manager is surlier than her staff.

- When calling, you dwell in hold-limbo for extended periods of time.

- Hold involves advertising or "informative" recordings that have nothing to do with your needs.

- The staff does not speak sufficient English to understand your order.*

- Two-star example: You get your car back from the shop and are told, "We fixed your problem, but you need to have your brakes fixed right away: they're not safe. We were too busy to do it today, so you should schedule an appointment. The first available is two weeks from next Thursday."

- Two-star culprits: Most doctors and their staffs provide two-star customer service. In my experience, ninety-seven percent.

- …And more culprits: Any bank I've ever been to is guilty of this type of service – and that's a lot of banks!

*Please do not misunderstand: I have always been sympathetic to immigrants and the difficulties they endure when they come here. In fact, I admire these people. I'm not saying they shouldn't come here until they've learned English, as I've heard some rednecks spout. What I am saying is, an employer who hires foreign workers who do not speak English has an obligation *to his customers* to make sure they learn at least basic English before they are promoted to a customer service position in his company.

Three-Star Service

When you think of three-star customer service, think of vanilla ice cream: plain, boring, average; doesn't offend anyone, also doesn't inspire a whole lot of loyalty. Three-star service is what you get most of the time. It neither disappoints nor impresses. It just "is."

Here's a three-star service provider that may surprise you – but it shouldn't: McDonald's.

"McDonald's," you ask? "If that's not one-star, what is?"

If that's your answer, then you're still confusing service with products. Sure, McDonald's food isn't all that good: with the exception of its salads, it's definitely one-star cuisine. But cheap quality, cheaply priced food is not how they grew to such enormity. It's consistency. As far as I can tell, no company has more consistency than the Golden Arches.

Why do we stop at McDonald's when there's so much better food out there? Perhaps because they're fast. The food is already made, but never cold. Service is quick. It seems like McDonald's workers are caffeine addicts. Ever notice? Compare that to Starbucks sometime. It's ironic.

In most parts of the country, with the exception of large cities or highway rest areas, you can also expect a sincere smile with your service.

Fast and friendly. Remarkably consistent. Each of those traits is part of the corporate culture: applicants are selected for the first two traits, then trained in them. Franchisees can lose their licenses if consistency flags.

McDonald's isn't the only three-star customer service provider out there, though. Let's go back to Starbucks. Nearly everything about that company is four-star. Four-dollar coffee. Fifteen-dollar coffee cups. Beautiful surroundings. *The New York Times* on sale. Comfortable chairs. Swanky locations. Internet access available to all (which, were it free, would be five-star customer service. They drop the ball here, big time).

But alas, they have a corporate culture, too, which has its customer service set quite low. Ask me for an example to support my claim, and I need search no further in my memory than today. While writing this book at Starbucks, the "barista" (a four-star term if ever there was one) made it a point not to crack a smile.

Like this worker, employees at Starbucks are often "too cool for school." Ask for a large, and you'll frequently be asked, "Venti?" The tone is ever-so-slightly disdainful. This from an $8/hour college dropout with a nose ring. Such things inspire cognitive dissonance.

And they're slow. It amazes me how a company that pushes high-test stimulants can have such low-energy workers. Are they banned from using their own wares?

Having indulged myself in this screed, I have to temper it a bit. While all of those things are true, that's not the complete picture. I'm often offered an extra shot of espresso free of charge when I'm there. No one hassles me for reading the *Times* when I'm waiting in line, though I rarely buy it. And I've had quite friendly service there, too. One clerk at my neighborhood branch (the grumpy barista's coworker) has become my bud. She calls me "The Teacher," and she starts making my "usual" as soon as I walk through the door. If I don't come around for a while, she asks where I've been the next time she sees me. All of that is certainly five-star service. Sadly, her Customer Service Ethic has not rubbed off on some of her coworkers.

While both McDonald's and Starbucks provide three-star service, the customer's perception of that service is quite different. McDonald's consistently fast and efficient service with a smile is more than you'd expect at a cheap burger joint, so the patron is often modestly impressed. Starbucks' high quality in other areas creates an expectation of high-quality service. But the service there is unpredictable, ranging from the rare five-star all the way down to two-, and occasionally one-star.* Its average of three-star service leaves the customer mildly disappointed.

In sum, Starbucks gets three stars because its standards are not set very high, not because its service is consistently bad. If you think management has no control over this, then please explain McDonald's.

*Inconsistency in products *or* service will harm a company, especially one that is growing as Starbucks is. To the observer who says, "What are you talking about? Look at that company's success! What harm?" I say, sure, Starbucks is growing successfully. But how much *more* successful would it be if its customer service consistently matched the quality of its products and "image?"

Discussion Questions

1. How does McDonald's consistently provide three-star service? What's their secret?

2. If McDonald's can provide service that is above the quality of its product, why doesn't every company? Why not Starbucks?

3. Name ten more companies of any type that provide three-star service: service that is neither good nor bad, and so is nothing you've even thought about before. Try to stretch yourself; think of companies that you work with, not just stores and restaurants.

4. Have you ever failed to smile at a customer? (Note: Even on the phone, people can "hear" whether or not you're smiling. More on that later.)

5. How would you rate your company's current level of customer service? At, below, or above three-star?

6. How do you think your boss rates it? And how does she feel about that rating?

7. How do you think your customers rate it?

Standards of three-star service include:

- You don't notice the service.
- Someone takes your order, serves your food, you eat; you leave. You have no complaints.

- You wait in a somewhat short line, make your purchase, get a half-hearted smile, and leave. Business as usual.

- You've been a regular customer for years, but few clerks remember your typical order, and no one has bothered to ever learn your name. You have no specific gripes, though sometimes this anonymity disappoints you.

- When you call, it takes quite a bit of listening and button pushing before you get a human.

- You are put on hold.

- Hold involves Muzak.

- Three-star example: At the service station, the mechanic fixes your car sufficiently. The estimate was reasonably close to your actual bill. You are told that your brakes will need repair within the next month. You can leave it for a few more days, or schedule to bring it back when it's more convenient.

Four-Star Service

Four-star service is unusual. It is often surprising, and leaves you feeling very good – very special – to have received it. Four-star service is excellent service. Typically you expect to pay through the nose for it. Fortunately, you don't always have to.

Think of three types of shopping experiences. Your typical mall is full of three-star service, and you think that's fine.

Then there are upscale malls with fancy, ultra-retail stores. With a few three- and five-star exceptions, you receive four-star service at the stores in this mall. Five-star service is what you would expect to find in the hoity-toitiest boutiques in your city's toniest neighborhoods.

I say "expect to find" for a reason: how many expensive boutiques, small art galleries, and the like actually provide exquisite customer service? My experience leads me to believe that too many fail their customers and themselves because, while the workers there are perfectly attentive and helpful, they also put on airs that can make the customer feel judged. And a five-star establishment would never peer down its nose at any customer, even subtly, no matter how shabby that customer's appearance or how bad her diction.

I'm not talking about the derision Julia Roberts encountered on Rodeo Drive in the movie *Pretty Woman*. That was no-star service. What I'm referring to is a much more subtle version of that. I think there's a certain type of person who actually appreciates a bit of snobbery with her service. This pretension doesn't do much for the rest of us, however.

So, excellent customer-service providers can knock themselves down a notch, to four-star, if their attitude is ever-so-slightly off. That's a negative. But four-star service is usually a positive. Think of the last time you entered an office building just as it started to rain, and the security guard smiled and said something like, "Perfect timing." That's nothing, half a breath's energy, but isn't it a great way to start your "business" together?

Of course, this friendly banter has to be followed up with courteous, knowledgeable service as you ask for directions to your appointment. If the building has strict rules, the guard has to be polite about asking for your name and who you're there to see, and careful not to offend as she asks you not to proceed until your appointment is confirmed. But if the entire experience is pleasant, you've probably just received four-star treatment.

Why not five-star? Keep in mind, four-star treatment is excellent. It is polished, professional, and hopefully warm; it is in the top ten percent of all service exchanges, and that's pretty special! But it has to blow you away before you consider it five-star.

Discussion Questions

1. If four-star is so good, why not stop there? Why aspire to be a five-star customer service provider?

2. If most companies cannot afford the staffing and training to be five-star across the board, can they still hit five-star standards in many of their practices?

3. What about this issue of warmth? How can an employer ever hope to instill that in his workers? (My answer: she can't. She has to hire already-warm people, then train them how to be efficient. The company culture has to be warm, and that starts with her treating her employees well).

Standards of four-star service include:

- When you walk into a shop, a clerk is there tidying up. She greets you warmly and says, "Can I help you find anything today?" A lot of people won't accept her offer, but she has made it and isn't pushy about it, which are the important parts.

    Personally, I can't stand shopping, so I always take a clerk up on this kind of offer. In a four-star establishment, I can recruit the clerk to guide me through *all* of my shopping needs.

- The manager is highly visible. He interacts frequently with the customer.
- A human answers the phone when you call. This person is warm and helpful. Rarely do you have to be passed on to a more qualified person to satisfy your request.
- The term "I'm sorry" is said often, and the speaker is clearly sincere.

- You also frequently hear, "I'm sure that's our mistake."
- Complaints are routinely handled to your satisfaction.
- Four-star example: Your mechanic calls you at the office to inform you that, while they've fixed your initial problem, they've also discovered that your brakes need repair. Would you like them fixed while the car is still up on the lift, so you can pick it up as scheduled?

Five-Star Service

I don't award this designation lightly. To me, nothing is rarer than five-star service (think the top one percent of all service exchanges), and that standard is worth protecting.

You know you're getting five-star service when, even on your first visit to a company, you are treated like a regular customer who has been spending a million dollars a week there for years.

"Wow! How can I measure up to that standard in the service I provide?" You ask. It's not easy. If you're an employer, it may appear impossibly expensive to maintain this as a constant level of performance. Roche Bros., for example, spends 50-75 *percent more* on payroll and training as its biggest competitor. But five-star service doesn't *have to* cost a company or organization more; remember the garbage man who places your empty barrels down gently. If providing this standard of service does end up costing more, companies usually make their investment back through the increased sales brought about by loyal customers and word-of-mouth.

Tiffany's is one company that really understands how to make five-star customer service work to its benefit. People will go out of their way to shop there. Give a gift from Tiffany's, and you'll get no end of Oos and Ahhs. Their stained glass and jewelry become family heirlooms. They may have fewer customers than other stores, but they certainly make up for that in profit margin: there is nothing inexpensive about a product from Tiffany's.

Did I say they may have fewer customers? Come to think of it, I don't think that's true. The Tiffany's stores I've gone to in Boston and New York are typically busier than other jewelers, including bottom-of-the-market Kay Jewlers. And Tiffany's certainly advertises very little. They don't have to: five-star products and service have had people buzzing for more than a century, giving them priceless word-of-mouth advertising.

The great thing about Tiffany's is that its customer service is as peerless as its wares. A decade ago, when I was a broke twenty-something shopping for Jane's engagement ring, I stopped by Tiffany's just to see what I couldn't afford, and maybe to pick up a pamphlet on selecting diamonds. I knew from growing up that nobody knew diamonds like Tiffany's. Word-of-mouth exposure.

In addition to a pamphlet, I was given a first-rate lesson in diamond selection by one of their salesclerks. Here I was, this kid in a polo shirt and jeans, receiving a first-rate, half-hour crash course from one of the most courteous customer service professionals I've ever met. He knew without asking that I wasn't going to buy from him; at the end of our talk, he even recommended where I should and should not go to get my money's worth, and to buy my girl the biggest, highest-quality rock I could on my modest budget.

Why did this man take the time to help me? Surely, while his store wasn't busy at the time (I got there before they opened and was the first one in), he could have blown me off to dust or something. I'm not sure; I'd have to ask him. But I think I know the answer: pride. Just like George Boldt, this man considered himself a top-rate customer service professional. Maybe he was getting practice on me, warming up his skills for a day of more fruitful sales after I'd gone. Maybe, as with Kelly the banker (whom you'll encounter later in this book), he figured he would invest his time in me then so that, after I'd built a business and become a best-selling author, I'd become his customer. Perhaps he suspected me of being an old-money scion who had the funds to spend there and didn't need to dress to impress. It's possible he saw something in me that I didn't see myself, something that said, "One day, this twerp is going to grow up and write a book about five-star customer service. Even if he forgets my name, he'll put Tiffany's in there if I treat him right."

Maybe. But I don't think any of that covers it. I think, rather, that this is standard operating procedure for Tiffany's. They're five-star across the board. They ooze class. This is just what they do, and their staff is proud to do it.

Standards of five-star service include:

- The same clerk helps you each time you visit his store, and he remembers your tastes and your name.
- Work is finished ahead of schedule.
- Your bill is less than you were quoted.
- The manager helps you himself, and wouldn't dream of accepting a tip. He thanks you for the opportunity to win your business.
- The phone is picked up by a friendly, literate human within the first two rings. This is the only person you have to deal with in order to resolve the issue for which you called. You never once hear the word "policy."
- Complaints are handled so well that you become a loyal customer for life, even if you weren't already.
- Five-star example: When your mechanic returns your car to your home or office, he tells you your brakes have been fixed along with your initial problem. He shows you your old brakes. Of course it costs more, so he asks if you would like to pay for the extra work now, or if you'd rather make arrangements.
- Another five-star example: The chef comes out from the kitchen to inquire as to how you enjoyed your

meal. He takes any recommendations to heart. While with you, he has an interaction with your waiter and treats this front-line professional warmly.

Summary

In terms we can all understand – our school days – think of service as follows:

- No-star service couldn't be worse. You are expelled from school, can't hold down a job as a clerk at Quickie Mart, and one day you die of an overdose in some back alley. Your "friends" rifle through your pockets, steal your shoes, and leave your corpse where it lies.

- One-star service is mildly terrible. You drop out of school as soon as the law allows, wash floors for a living, and supplement that income dealing pot out of the trunk of your beat-up old car, which you sometimes have to live in.

- Two-star service has plenty of room for improvement. You don't really take to trade school, and hold a succession of jobs in second-rate businesses, with abusive bosses who don't really miss you when you quit.

- Three-star service is good. A grade of "B" in school. You're going to college.

- Four-star service is excellent. An "A" average. Your parents brag about you to their friends.
- Five-star service is phenomenal. An "A+" average. A 4.0. The Dean's List. A Rhodes scholarship. The mayor gives you the key to your town when you return home from your top-notch college.

With three-star service, you'll suffer few complaints. You should also expect no loyalty.

When you provide four-star service, people will be impressed. They'll almost certainly come back. Some will even tell their friends. You should feel proud of yourself if this is your standard of service.

When you establish your reputation as a five-star customer service provider, all but the most spoiled few will gush to their friends, family, co-workers, and absolute strangers about how special – strike that, how *cherished* – they feel as your customer. Even if you stop advertising, your business will continue to thrive for some time to come. At this point, word-of mouth is your best marketeer.

From The Trenches:

I Quit – No, Really!

Here's one that happened recently, and it still blows my mind.

Coiné Corporate Training is a very agile organization (read: small), and we move our main office from time to time as we outgrow our latest space. So when we decided to up and move yet again, the natural first step was to call our various utilities and let them know about it. We called the telephone company, the electric company... and our cable Internet provider. Cue ominous music.

Guess what? You can't just opt out of using the cable company. Our office manager seemed to have no luck canceling service. Peeved, I made the next call myself.

Them: "We can't take requests for interruption of service by phone."

Me: "Huh? No, we quit. We don't want to play anymore. I'm taking my ball and going home."

Them: "Sorry, that's not possible. You'll have to fax your request to our termination department."

Me (thinking): Excuse me? I beg your pardon? Is this customer service? Is it even *legal?*

Now, I have a couple of issues before we even start. Like, why is my home account, with the same exact company and service, "only" $50 a month when my business costs me $200? Companies routinely gouge other companies because they can, and that's just wrong. In the Land of Small Businesses, which our great republic is, I can't imagine how this is ethical, conducive to growth, or even allowed by our legislators. That gouging is one-star customer service if ever I've seen it.

That's the first thing. The second is, it's the new millennium. How come we're still using faxes?

These gizmos were great in the 1980's, even the early 90's. Remember that cheap, flimsy, glossy paper they used to use? The kind that smudged, and that was really hard to read? It was like magic!

But now we've got scanners, and the Internet. Rather than tying up a phone line (and either unplugging the main phone or paying another monopoly for a dedicated line), we can scan and send, without even dialing a number, without the threat of a busy signal – and with the guarantee that, if you can learn to use the added features of your email, you can check to be sure it arrived at the recipient's desk, and even when it was opened. Now that's Twenty-First Century cool!

Discussion Questions

1. Does your company take advantage of other companies to whom it sells, through higher prices than what it charges to the general public? If yes, how do you live with yourself? And is that serving your customers, or abusing them and actually begging them to flee to a cheaper and more ethical alternative as soon as the opportunity presents itself?

2. Does your company use faxes… ever? Routinely? Unavoidably? If so, is that the best way to serve your customers? Is there a better way?

Back to the cable company. Here's my question: If I don't want to use your company's service or pay you for it, and if I unplug your line (demonstrating that I'm done), that should be the end of it. And if I'm kind enough to call and let you know about it, well then, now we're *really* getting official. I mean, how can a company tell me that unless I jump through their hoop, I can't quit? That quitting the customer-vendor relationship is not up to me alone? I need permission to opt out of our relationship? Come on, this is not high school romance!

Am I missing something here?

I understand that, if the cable company allows termination by phone, a disgruntled employee can place a call and screw your entire operation up for hours, until you call to straighten it out (and who knows, it would probably take until two weeks from Monday, between eight and one (please wait around) to get a switch flipped in the local headquarters, in order to restore service – with a "service charge" to boot.) However, if that same disgruntled employee would just show a little gumption, she could send a fax, and get the same result.

(By the way: There is no such thing as a "Service Charge." They should call it an "Insult Charge.")

Hmn seems I woke up on the wrong side of the coffee maker this morning. I had meant for this section to be a paragraph. But I'll tell you, if your company doesn't make quitting automatic, it's not really serving anyone but itself. And that only in the short-term. I promise, such alienation of your customers will assure you've lost their loyalty. They'll drop you like a hot potato as soon as a better offer comes along.

Actually, this same thing happened with a bank I used while living in California. When I moved to Boston, I let my account drop down to zero. There was probably about $1.60 in it at the time (my average balance – my motto that year was "Surf more, work less"), and I didn't bother withdrawing that.

Of course, I assumed the bank would devour my remaining funds for its service charge, then close my account. Instead, they charged me their fee for three months. In their eyes, I ended up owing them about $36. And they wouldn't take it off of my credit report, even after I paid that fee, and wrote a letter to the bank president asking for them to do so. I suffered seven years for their policy.

Imagine if the Gap charged you for shirts you didn't buy, just because you had bought from them in the past? And when you called to ask them to desist, they told you you'd have to send them a fax?

The lesson here is that there are some not-so-subtle hints that a customer can use to let you know that he is not your customer anymore. Like no longer buying from you, for instance. In the spirit of good customer service, you would be well advised to take those hints.

Discussion Questions

1. How do policies like the cable company's and the bank's serve the customer?

2. How do they serve the company? All ranting aside, they may have some purpose that helps the company to run more smoothly. Try to imagine how.

3. In the long run, do such practices help or hurt a business' growth?

4. How would you feel if you had to send that fax, or suffer bad credit for not officially closing your bank account?

5. Does your company have policies that are in any way similar to these?

6. How do these practices help your company?

7. Is there any other way you can think of that your company could achieve the purpose of the practices described in question 5 without alienating your customers?

3

FIVE STAR CUSTOMER SERVICE: FORMAL OR FRIENDLY?

"I like to be treated like a queen."
-Marion Southard

Is Five-Star Customer Service supposed to be formal, or should it be friendly? The short answer is, "Yes."

You expect to receive five-star treatment from a five-star hotel, and usually you do. You don't expect to find it at the hardware store, but in rare instances you will. So the real answer to the question, "Formal or Friendly?" is, "Either." Or, "Both." In their own ways, formal service and very warm service can each be five-star.

Five-star service should be respectful and formal, and also welcoming. Or it can be warm and hospitable, while also courteous.

If the service you receive is respectful and formal, but does not make you feel welcome, then guess what? I don't care if they dry you off by hand after a hot bath and *dress* you: it's still only four-star. Keep this rule of thumb in mind:

"Not welcoming? Not five-star."

However, just because service makes you feel like part of the family doesn't make it five-star, either; as much as I love them, my family has never given me five-star service! So warmth doesn't automatically qualify service as five-star, either. Not by a long shot.

What's the secret, then? The thing about five-star service is, it's in the eye of the beholder. *If* you feel intensely special, *if* you have no complaints whatsoever, *if* you wish the whole world worked this way, but *if* you also realize that it only does about one percent of the time... *then* you're likely experiencing five-star customer service.

An ongoing discussion with my mother inspired this chapter. As I share throughout this book, it makes me feel very good to get sincerely warm, inclusive treatment from customer service professionals. I like the kind of connection that makes me feel as though I've made a friend, even though it's possible that I'll never seen this person again. That to me is a hallmark of outstanding customer service, and I'm very critical of "stiff" yet flawless service.

My Mom, on the other hand, likes to be treated like royalty from time to time. She was raised a Boston blueblood, and though she's the kindest and friendliest person you'll ever meet, and while she's very comfortable in her middle-class skin, she still has these upper-crust, Old New England standards that she lives by. Because of this, Mom and I couldn't have more opposite definitions of five-star service.

…But you know what? We're both right. Here are a few examples to illustrate what I mean.

There's a Reason They Call It "The Ritz"

Marion and Ed Southard, my Mom and stepfather, are "snow birds:" they live half the year in Fairfield, Connecticut and the other half in Naples, Florida. Now, both are exclusive towns, but Naples has the distinction of being home to more millionaires per capita than any other spot in the US (which does *not* include the Southards, sadly for us all). So, there is no shortage of deluxe hotels, restaurants, clubs, catered dinner parties, galleries, and shops for them to enjoy.

Mom's favorite spot in all of Naples is the Ritz-Carlton, on Vanderbilt Beach. She says that from the moment she drives in, she is treated like a queen. The doorman opens her car door for her, everyone says, "Yes, ma'am," the waiters brush the crumbs off of their table, but do not disturb her party as they eat… it's heavenly to Mom. And I like that kind of treatment, too. Who wouldn't?

My friend Mike says the same thing. "Naples? My wife and I spent a week at the Ritz down there, and it was amazing. Everyone on staff has 'I'm sorry' money to spend – even the maids will say, 'Oh, your slippers were not by your bed? Here's a coupon for a free breakfast. I'm sorry, sir.'" Mike tells me that week at the Naples Ritz was one of the best he's ever had.

That's why they call it The Ritz, after all: it's "Ritzy." The service there is formal, exactingly professional; all you could possibly hope for. It's five-star, without a doubt.

Discussion Questions:

1. "Of course the Ritz is five-star," you say. "They can afford to be, with the prices they charge." Is it even remotely possible to learn anything from a company that can charge such a premium for its services?

2. How could you instill some of the customer-service practices of a firm like Ritz-Carlton in your own organization, without spending Ritz-Carlton money to do it?

What happens when the service is flawless, yet the customer feels strangely under-appreciated? For the answer to that question, we go to the sunny Caribbean island of Aruba.

Missing the Fifth Star

For our honeymoon, Jane and I spent a week each on two Caribbean islands, Jamaica and Aruba. While we stayed at a nice resort in Jamaica, and loved every minute of our time there, the service wasn't much to brag about – a bit lax, overall. Through their example, our hosts taught us how to live by the credo, "No problem, Mon" – something our Yankee souls really needed, to be sure, though it took several days for us to get used to. Most people were intensely warm and friendly, though, and overall it was perhaps the best vacation either of us has ever had.

Aruba was different in every way, from its climate to its social norms to the plentiful Dunkin Donuts and Subways to the polite efficiency of *all* of its residents. Really, we found it uncanny how *every single* native we met over the course of that week was equally courteous and helpful. ...But we noticed after a few days that they weren't warm, as the Jamaicans were. They smiled, but more out of habit – more from the mouth, less from the eyes. They were professional and proud of the service they provided. They didn't genuinely love us.

Not that they had to; you certainly can't compel your workers to love their customers. But that's one key difference between four- and five-star service. Aruba gave nothing but completely excellent and efficient service. We had no complaints over seven days, and the people we met, even just passersby we asked for directions, were quite helpful. Overall, we enjoyed our stay. However, we really missed Jamaica the whole time we were in Aruba.

Five-star customer service isn't all about perfection. It's also about warmth and goodwill. Jamaica gave us nowhere near five-star service; it was probably two-star overall (except when the activities directors failed to show up at all for scheduled events). But, while the service in Aruba left nothing tangible to be desired, it was that intangible extra, sincere warmth, that brought the service there down a notch, to four-star.

Discussion Questions

1. Jane and I didn't have any specific complaints with the service in Aruba, and we were actually blown away that an entire island-nation could be so courteous. Shouldn't I lighten up and give them the fifth star?

2. How is it that we enjoyed the two-star service of Jamaica better than the four-star service of Aruba?

This is not a book about how you can turn your organization into another Ritz-Carlton. For one thing, there aren't enough people in the world with the kind of money to keep more than a handful of Ritz-quality hotels in business; most of us will be lucky to get out of Motel 6 and into someplace with cotton towels. But we want five-star service, too, if we can get it. And if we can't get it in Aruba, perhaps we should give Williamsburg, Virginia a try.

Ernestine

I chose my college, William and Mary, for a number of reasons, from academic excellence and the quality of the swim team, to milder Virginia weather and the unrivaled beauty of the campus. I also went there looking for a slight change in culture. Having grown up a Connecticut Yankee, I thought it high time I experience a little Southern Hospitality.

I wasn't disappointed. From my first day on campus, my fellow students waved and smiled from across the street – even though I'd never met them. Indeed, the first time this happened, I looked behind me, certain their wave was meant for someone else. It wasn't.

Also on that first day, I made an extraordinary friend. Ernestine was this big, always jolly lady who swiped our meal cards as we entered the cafeteria. Every lunch and dinner, she would greet me with a boisterous, "Hey, baby!" We'd chat for a minute if the line was slow, and then she'd greet her next pal when I moved on.

This went on for five years, until I graduated and left town. I didn't give it much thought, until I returned for my five-year reunion with my then-girlfriend, Jane. The first morning in The Burg, we walked into one of the many local pancake houses, when what did I hear from across the room but, "*BA*-by!"

I recognized the voice instantly. It was Ernestine, and I can't even tell you how happy she seemed to see me! It made the entire trip down from Boston worth it just to see my friend Ernestine and to know she still remembered me.

We caught up a bit. She clearly loved Jane, which meant almost as much to me as when my Mom had given Jane the thumbs up two years earlier. Ernestine told me how proud she was that I was an executive, with a secretary and everything. "Only 26! My, my, you've done great for yourself, sweetheart." I was always Sweetheart, Baby, and Darlin' to Ernestine. And, Yankee or no, I never once found it patronizing, fake, or hokey. I ate it up.

Marriott managed The College cafeterias when I was there. I have no question that they benefited from employing Ernestine. I know I kept my meal plan my two senior years (ehem…) only because of her; my apartment had a perfectly good kitchen, but it went largely unused in part because I just didn't want to hurt Ernestine's feelings. I wonder how many other students paid their $800 or $1,200 dollars per semester for the same reason? I guarantee, Marriott did not pay Ernestine much over minimum wage: the Williamsburg job market doesn't operate that way. But clearly pay wasn't what inspired Ernestine to provide the atmosphere of hospitality that made my trips to the cafeteria so special.

Discussion Questions

1. How was Ernestine's warm hospitality five-star customer service?

2. How did Marriott benefit from her Customer Service Ethic?

3. How did Ernestine benefit from her attitude at work?

4. How did Marriott's customers (the students) benefit from Ernestine's Ethic?

5. Do you see a relationship among the last three questions?

6. How do *you* measure up to Ernestine, as a customer-service provider?

7. What could you do differently to better meet the high standard of Ernestine's customer service, without being fake or becoming a different person?

About four years ago, Ernestine passed away. I missed the funeral, but several *thousand* others did not. Here she was, just a minimum-wage worker, a high school graduate, being honored and lauded by so many of the people whose lives she had enriched over the years. The president of William & Mary eulogized her. Public figures, accomplished professionals, and business leaders stood shoulder to shoulder with her family and local friends to see her off to a certain berth in Heaven. Ernestine had touched us all.

* * * * *

The thing about customer service is, it's like apples and oranges: which do you prefer? They're both tasty, both healthy. Life would be less rich if you could only have one or the other. I'd certainly hate to have to choose.

My Mom loves the Ritz: she enjoys apples. She doesn't feel right when a cashier like Ernestine is so effusively familiar. At first meeting, my Mom — and most Yankees – would probably find Ernestine "fake." I can hear it now: "What's she on?" or, "What do you think that lady wants?" All folks like my Mom want is to be pampered lavishly and left to themselves. In Mom's defense, I enjoy my privacy and anonymity as well; I can see part of her point, anyway.

I certainly appreciate the Ritz brand of customer service, but I'll choose one Ernestine over twelve valets any day. I'm an orange guy. Like my mother, I expect five-star service to provide for – no, to *anticipate* – my desires, and to be exceedingly polite, gracious even. But I want a little soul thrown into the mix for good measure. I don't just want to attend a gala event; I want the hosts to make me feel that I made their night by coming.

As far as I can see, we're both right. What's your take on this debate?

From The Trenches:

Five-Star Service in the Unlikeliest of Places

Call me ill-informed, but to me gas is gas is gas.

My criteria for choosing where to fuel up are straightforward: what's cheapest, and do they pump it for you? Strangely, those two usually go hand-in-hand.

I have no loyalty to brand or service station – with one exception. Whenever I'm in the neighborhood, I make sure to fill my tank at a little station in Quincy, Massachusetts called, creatively enough, Quincy Gas.

My wife, Jane, and I stumbled upon this spot purely by accident one day after visiting our friend. We needed gas, we stopped….and we experienced five-star customer service, in the unlikeliest of places.

Quincy is a working-class town. This station isn't too pretty to look at. But the clerk made up for all that.

First, he asked us if we had been there before. We had not. So he explained their contest. If you guess how much gas your tank will take, right down to the penny, then your fill-up is free. He told us they give away about two tanks each week.

We guessed; we didn't win. But as consolation, the clerk offered us each a piece of Baklava, fresh from the owner's stepfather's kitchen. It was the best Baklava we'd ever had, so delicious that I wondered why they weren't in the business of selling pastries, and giving gas away, instead.

Jane and I love what we call "service extras," and this experience really intrigued us. So we asked some questions.

Who thought of this contest? They'd been doing it for years. It started as the suggestion of a regular customer's. He was a wise guy, and was just joking. He said to the clerk, "If I guess it right, are you gonna buy my gas?" To his surprise, the clerk took him up on the offer. The man lost that time, but he's won a few times in the years since.

Who pays? Not this clerk, or his coworkers. The owner, Harvey Kertzman, picks up the tab. But we found it interesting that Harvey so readily bought into a customer-inspired idea, and that his hourly-wage clerk felt the freedom to undertake such a project without checking first.

We asked about the longevity of the staff. Most gas stations we frequent are staffed by immigrants and high school kids. This is generally a first job. The turnover is pretty high because employees quickly find better-paying work elsewhere.

The clerk we spoke to that day said that Harvey pays his guys several dollars an hour more than the going rate. He also treats them well in other ways. When this particular clerk's grandmother was hospitalized the year before, he missed several days of work, but that Friday his check was the same size as always.

Of course, that goes both ways. The clerk wasn't the type to accept handouts; over the next two weeks, he picked up several of Harvey's shifts without accepting pay. But at his insistence, not Harvey's.

Discussion Questions

1. Managers: what would you do in a similar situation?

2. What would your employee do in response?

Five-star values permeate a company, and go well beyond customer service.

I caught up with Harvey shortly before finishing this book, and we had a very interesting conversation. He told me all about the businesses that he runs and has run in the past. He showed me the newspaper clipping about the guitarist/ singer he'd sometimes hire to serenade his customers. We discussed how he'd like to teach classes to attendants from other service stations, because no one else knows the first thing about customer service in that field anymore. And he shared with me his favorite saying. "Have a grateful day," he tells people in lieu of goodbye.

"It's not a religious thing, or from a ten-step program or anything," he assured me. "I just want to get people thinking. Because we should be grateful for every day that we're here.

"It's great to hear that when I'm somewhere else, too. I can be cashing out at a store twenty miles away, and I'll say, 'Have a grateful day' to the cashier. Someone behind me will say, 'That's what they say at that gas station in Quincy!' I get a big kick out of that. I want to see how far I can spread that message: fifty miles? Two hundred miles? The world?" He laughs, but I know he's only half-joking.

"I've made my fortune. I don't work for money anymore. I do it to meet people, and maybe to make one customer in a hundred stop and think about that saying, 'Have a grateful day.' It doesn't matter if I'm selling gas, cigarettes, or renting Budget trucks. Our commitment to customer service is the same."

Harvey may not be in a five-star industry, but that doesn't matter to him in the least. To Harvey Kertzman of Quincy Gas, five-star customer service, and the goodwill that goes right along with it, is nothing more or less than a matter of pride.

Discussion Questions

1. What does the owner, Harvey, gain financially by offering this contest?

2. What does he gain by paying his staff more than necessary?

3. Is it worth it? Think in terms of dollars, not Karma.

4. What does he gain by treating his employees well?

5. What advantages does Harvey get over his competition through his management style?

6. What lessons about your own work can you learn from this story?

7. Take a moment to make a list of some fresh ideas you can add to your daily activities. Focus on things that will include and engage your customers.

4

"WHAT WOULD GEORGE DO?"

You (if you're smart)

You've been introduced to the Customer Service Ethic, which is the philosophy behind everything you will ever learn in customer service.

You've had the five stars explained to you, with plenty of examples to flesh out the differences. And we have discussed the seeming conflict between warm and formal service.

You should have a pretty good basis for judging other customer service encounters now. If you really take what you've learned so far to heart, you should also begin to be able to evaluate your own behavior as a customer service professional.

So now that you've got the foundation and the frame of your five-star castle built, it's time to equip you with the tools to improve your own job performance.

First off, you need a role model. Choose a person who represents unstinting five-star customer service for your company. My first recommendation is that you choose somebody you know, preferably the leader of your company (but only if it's appropriate!). Her entire time with Roche Bros., Jane used to say to herself, "What would Pat and Bud do?"

Pat and Bud Roche founded the company back in the 1950's. They still ran the firm for years after Jane joined. They set the original standard of customer service excellence that made Roche Bros. such a symbol of quality in Eastern Massachusetts. During their entire fifty-some-odd-year tenure, they never varied from their commitment to customer service. Whenever Jane had a customer service dilemma to solve, she would ask herself this question, and often the solution simply presented itself.

Legal Sea Foods also has a charismatic leader in its CEO and president, Roger Berkowitz. Roger is actively involved in every aspect of that company, and it is his leadership, as with the Roche brothers, that sets and helps maintain the entire company's commitment to customer service excellence. If I worked for Legal, I'd make that my mantra: "What would Roger do?" I think most people in the company are pretty clear on the answer to that question.

Does your company have a charismatic, service-obsessed leader? Be careful about this: if it doesn't, you're going to get yourself in a lot of trouble by asking yourself what she would do. If this person allows sub-par service performance on the job, choose someone else! (Don't worry; there are a lot of excellent company leaders who aren't customer service gurus. Hopefully, not choosing your founder/CEO/president, etc. won't hurt her feelings.)

Another thing to consider is, both of the companies I mentioned are privately owned. There is a world full of companies without a charismatic leader, or with new leadership every couple of years, or with distant, nameless, and faceless leaders. You can recruit a namesake for this catchphrase from outside of your company.

Personally, I ask myself, "What would Jane do?" Yes, my wife is my customer service guru, and I'm not afraid to admit it.

I recommend you use George Boldt, if that works for you. Whenever you're uncertain, just ask yourself, "What would George do?"

If none of these people works for you, then by all means, you are welcome to start saying, "What would Ted do?" I'd be honored.

Whoever you decide on, "What would _____ do?" is a phrase you and your colleagues should incorporate into your daily conversations. It will serve to help you make tough calls.

It will inspire you not to cut corners; indeed, to go several extra miles to ensure your customers are more satisfied than they ever thought they could be.

Discussion Questions

1. Who should serve as the namesake for this catchphrase in your company?

2. Why did you choose that person? What does he/she represent to you?

3. How do you feel about this catchphrase, anyway? Is it going to be useful? Fun? Hokey? Remember, if you don't buy into it, it's not going to help anyone.

4. How will the rest of your coworkers, who have not read this book, react to this new slogan when (if) you start sharing it with them?

5. How can you involve these others to make the slogan catch on and get results company-wide?

"What Would George Do?"

This is your new mantra. Ask it of yourself all day long. Ask it of your colleagues. And really give it some thought. Because it's the company of owner-minded professionals that will win the customer service battle day after day after inspiring day.

From The Trenches:

We Hate Our Customers

I've been an avid gardener my whole life, so when Jane and I bought our first house several years ago, I started spending most of my (modest) disposable income on flowers, shrubs, and flowering trees in order to spruce it up.

My nursery of choice was a high-end place in Milton, a somewhat chichi suburb of Boston not far from our town. If the dogwoods and cherry trees I bought were a bit pricier, I found that their superior quality and the sound gardening advice I got there more than made up for the extra money spent.

Milton is also one of our favorite local towns, nestled in the middle of our favorite Boston-area nature preserve, the Blue Hills. We'd often go out of our way to visit this particular nursery just for the pleasant scenery on the way there and back. Once there, of course, we'd make a purchase more often than not.

I had been a regular customer there for about three years, and must have spent a few thousand dollars all told – which, on a private school teacher's salary, was a tremendous amount of money.

So one day, Jane and I were driving by this nursery when, pregnant as she was, she had to find a lady's room – and pronto! Naturally, I pulled into the nursery.

The only problem was, the nursery had a new policy: "No Public Rest Rooms." They had a single-use restroom in the front; I knew because I'd used it before. But this time the door was locked with a key, and the door sported that new, unwelcoming sign. The clerk upheld the policy; when I spoke to the manager, he denied Jane use of the restroom as well. We ended up driving another five miles to get to the next business.

Discussion Questions

1. What do you think of this story? Was the nursery right in its new policy? A lot of companies have similar policies. How do you feel about them?

2. Why does a company choose to open or close its restrooms to the public and its customers? Both decisions have advantages and disadvantages. Remembering the topic is five-star customer service, which policy is best for a company to have?

3. Were there any additional circumstances that the clerk or manager should have taken into consideration when enforcing the policy?

4. "Policy is policy/the rules are the rules." Do you agree or disagree with this statement?

5. Was this five-star customer service? If not, how many stars would you rate it?

6. What should Jane and I have done following this episode? Should we have written a letter to the owner? Taken our business elsewhere? Forgotten about the whole thing, and just made sure we went to the bathroom before shopping there?

Fortunately, Jane didn't have an accident on the way to a friendlier establishment. And also fortunately for us, after just a little searching I uncovered a modest nursery in our own town, Stoughton Nursery. The prices are lower, the quality of the plants just as good, and the best part? The owner's son delivers my bushes and trees at no extra expense. He won't take a tip, and he even helps me get the bigger trees into their holes. That's the kind of service excellence this book is all about.

Five-star customer service, at less expense to boot. I'll never shop anywhere else. And because I'm such a satisfied customer, I've referred several of my neighbors and friends, one of whom even lives only two miles from the Milton nursery.

From The Trenches:

"My job is to make your job easier."
- Ted Coiné

"You know, I think you're the only
person in business today
who really means that."
- Alan Dempsey, Legal Sea Foods

Alan laughed when he said that, but he was joking about the truth. There is nothing less common than someone who truly puts his client's needs before his own. Make it a habit and sooner or later we'll see your smiling face on the cover of Fortune magazine.

That line I gave Alan is one of our big slogans at Coiné Corporate Training. I share it with clients all the time, and encourage my staff to as well. I think it sums up one of the most important aspects of the Customer Service Ethic in action: that a five-star customer service professional is in business to be helpful. When his job involves working with other companies, his job is absolutely to make his counterparts at these companies less harried.

My teachers and I often go into companies for stretches of three, six, nine months or more. We could easily be a thorn in the side of the managers with whom we work. Further, not all of these managers agree with their company leadership that our training is even necessary; as many as a quarter of the low- and mid-level managers we work with see our classes as an intrusion, missing the long view that better-trained workers are more productive and thus make the managers' jobs less stressful.

Under these conditions – and also just because, as a matter of pride, I couldn't do it any other way – we take great pains to keep a low profile in any company kind enough to hire us on. This practice is professional, without doubt. It is also smart. After all, we want to be invited back for more business, and we want our existing clients to give us rave reviews when prospective clients call for a reference.

In every interaction we have with our clients, both on-site and from our office (via telephone and email), we strive to live up to our motto. And often it's the little things that make the difference. For instance, if a client asks to cancel class on a busy day – if it's a retail spot, then perhaps the week before Christmas – we accommodate them as a matter of course, and so long as we've had 24 hours' notice to inform (and hopefully reassign) the teacher, we tag the missed class on to the end.

I am often amazed at how grateful managers are when we tell them we're happy to oblige in this way. But I know why they are: too many other service providers would make a stink over this type of thing. They'd hem and haw.

> "It will cost us money!" (True enough. What can you do?).

> "It's against policy." (Who makes policy? Get that person on the phone).

> "We can do it, but we'll have to charge you for the class." (Uh... that's customer service?)

Discussion Questions

1. Would your customers say you make their jobs easier? (Or their shopping experience, or... you get the idea).

2. How accommodating are you when a customer has a special request?

3. Do special orders upset you?* Do you take them in stride? Or do you look at a customer with a particular need as someone who is giving you the chance to show off your stuff?

*Remember that old Burger King jingle?

> Hold the pickles,
> Hold the lettuce,

> Special orders don't upset us,
> All we ask is that you let us
> Have it your way.

Burger King was selling customer service, not hamburgers. As for how much market share it captured from McDonald's and why... I'm going to have to save that for another book.

5

WHO WINS AN ARGUMENT?

"No one ever wins an argument with his customer."
Steve Coiné

The quote above is one of the most basic concepts in customer service. However, as a great mind once said of common sense, basic customer service is the rarest of commodities.

Written In Stone

When I was a boy, my mother always took me shopping at Stew Leonard's, a tiny dairy store in Norwalk, Connecticut. Inside, at least when I was three, all you could buy there was milk and eggs. I don't think they even had cheese or butter at that point.

Needless to say, the inside of the store didn't do much for me. But Stew was no dummy: he knew that moms are going to do their shopping where their children are happiest, and that was Stew Leonard's.

Out in front of his small store were three things that really caught a young kid's attention. The first was the petting zoo. Stew always had a menagerie of sheep, goats, chickens, ducks, and sometimes even a couple of cows, together in two pens connected by a bridge. Wow! We could always feed the animals, and of course it didn't take Stew long to add bread to his offerings. Mom would buy two loaves of bread, one for the family and one for the two of us to feed the animals.

There was a silo out in front of the store, which in the early 70's dwarfed the rest of his building. And, most important to me today (though not as impressive back then), there was a boulder, at least eight feet high, with these words inscribed on it:

Rule #1
The Customer is Always Right.

Rule #2
If the Customer is Ever Wrong,
Reread Rule #1!

As you can see, my training in customer service started early. But enough about me. Let's talk about what you, the customer service professional, get out of this.

Discussion questions:

1. Why is this inscription written in stone?

2. Why is it positioned at the entrance?

3. What do you think the inscription on the rock in front of Stew Leonard's means to that company?

4. What does it mean to you in your job?

5. Of course customers are wrong. They're people! ...Right?

All throughout my childhood, that little dairy store grew and grew. By the time I graduated from high school, the multiple roofs over various additions had made the "huge" silo look like a toy. Today, Stew Leonard's is proud to advertise itself as "The World's Largest Dairy Store" – although they sell a whole lot more than just dairy these days. They also have expanded to a couple of other locations, and are just as popular there as in Norwalk.

Stew Leonard's is truly a business to admire. It has been chronicled in countless business textbooks, magazine articles, news programs ...Stew even spoke on a Business English tape I used to use with my foreign executive students.

But what is their secret to ongoing success? Stew Leonard's didn't grow because its milk tasted richer than the grocery store's across the street (which has long since gone out of business). Its eggs were no bigger *or* cheaper than anyone else's. Certainly the animals helped, but they didn't make the Leonard family wealthy.

So what brought about their tremendous success? It was that rock. Or more accurately, what it represents. If Stew Leonard knew anything, it was that you can never win a fight with your customer. And you can never do enough to make your customer feel special, welcome, important, necessary; like the boss. Do that and your business will grow immensely, just as Stew Leonard's has.

I highly recommend you take a trip to Stew Leonard's if you are ever within 100 miles of Norwalk, Connecticut. As a customer service professional, soak it in. Don't just shop: observe. Spend the afternoon. Better yet, call ahead, and book a tour. Management loves to teach the customer service gospel to other business leaders.

But the specifics of how Stew runs his grocery store aren't really important to this book. The key to his story is that rock, and the Customer Service Ethic that inspired it.

Discussion Questions:

1. How can you apply the two rules on Stew Leonard's rock to your job and your company's operation?

2. What practices do you already follow that live up to Stew Leonard's standards?

3. What are you not presently doing in your job that you should be?

Stew Leonard's is the good side of the lesson of this chapter. Prepare yourself for the Dark Side....

You're right! ...And your competitor is grateful.

We live around the corner from a nice little open-air mall. There's an inexpensive Italian restaurant there, part of a large Boston-based chain. It's the only place to eat within walking distance of our house, the food isn't half bad, and its patio is a nice spot to relax after a long day's work. For a few years we were more or less on their meal plan when the weather warmed up.

The service is moderately polite, though not that good. That's okay: after years in the foodservice field, I know quite well how it works. This is a first job for most talented waiters, a place to cut your teeth before moving on to someplace more exacting and more profitable. We didn't expect all that much when we went there.

I have a favorite dish at this chain, broiled salmon on a bed of wilted spinach. "Wilted" means the cook prepares the salmon, then throws the spinach into the buttery pan and stirs it around until it is just barely cooked. That's how I'd gotten it for two years, until a new manager shook things up a bit in the kitchen. One day, my spinach came to me completely uncooked. I asked to speak to the manager.

Don't misunderstand me: this is not a book on cuisine. If the food at a restaurant isn't prepared to your liking, that affects its stars for the quality of the food, but it has no bearing on the quality of service. And all we're interested in right now is service.

It's the manager's response to my request for wilting that makes this tale germane to the discussion of customer service. As politely as he could, he argued with me over the preparation of my meal.

His first mistake was that he clearly did not believe me when I explained I'd been getting more-cooked spinach for two years at his restaurant. No customer likes to be called a liar, even if he has to infer it.

The manager went on to educate me. Mistake number two. "Wilted means…" I'll spare you a repeat of the details. Suffice it to say, he and I agreed in theory on the meaning of wilting. The fact that he forced me to sit through his explanation was exasperating.

"I'd be happy to take it back and have it cooked for you. I'm sorry you don't like it wilted." Strike three! After all of the lecturing, he insisted on being right, almost taunting me in the process. Another customer might have been infuriated and stormed out. I try not to let bad service perturb me anymore, though, so I just let it go.

This manager insisted on being right. To him, that was the most important thing he took out of the exchange with me, his customer. The fact that I clearly *thought* I was right didn't faze him in the least. As far as he was concerned, he won the battle of the definition of "wilted." He walked away a winner.

Ah, but what did he lose? No one's going to recruit him to manage their fancier, better-paying business, as happened to George Boldt (and three times to me) because of the excellent customer service he provided. His company doesn't get my business all fall, winter, and spring because, without that patio, I'll drive a little farther for better service at the same price. And his company also doesn't get named in this book: no free advertising. If you notice, I take pains whenever possible only to name the companies that do it right.

What I got that day was two-star service (Jane, the protective mother bear, says it was one-star). Indeed, we finally gave up on the place altogether, patio be damned. That whole company gets the thumbs down, as far as I'm concerned – all because of one poorly trained manager.

Discussion Questions

1. What *should* the manager have done when I requested more wilting?

2. What could the manager have done the next time he saw me coming?

3. What would you do in this situation?

4. Do you have any similar experiences?

5. Have you ever corrected a customer? How well did that go over? Did it make you feel better? How do you think the customer felt?

When you and your customer have a disagreement, neither of you wins: your competitor does. Remember: if your customer is ever wrong, reread Stew Leonard's Rule #1.

From The Trenches:

"It's Policy."
Another way to say,
"Please Take Your Business Elsewhere."

A smart customer knows that a company can do anything it wants; if an employee isn't authorized to bend a rule, there's always someone higher up the chain of command who is. People make policy, so those same people (or their bosses) can change it.

It is vital, therefore, that your leadership train its front-line staff, its customer service professionals, to realize this and act accordingly.

I'm still embarrassed-by-association when I think of the first school I worked for as a teacher. The administration stood (actually, *still stands*) behind all-holy "Policy" in denying any form of refund or special consideration, no matter the situation.

I was "just" a teacher, so I had no say in how the school was run outside of my classroom. We teachers were blameless. But still, we were witness to shabby ethics, if not outright dishonesty. And poor ethics make for poor customer service. There's just no getting around that.

Over the years quite a number of my students came to class and shared their frustration, because school "Policy" prohibited the administration from giving a refund if a student's car did not pick her up at the airport. Or if she'd paid ahead for six months, but had to cut her studies short because her mother was ill. And no, she could not defer the rest of her course for several months and then return to finish, either.

The way they handled problems with housing? "Policy" prohibited the school from compensating host families if their students didn't show up as scheduled, but "Policy" held that the student still paid, no matter what. Basically, that made two losers, with the school as the winner: money for nothing.

I wonder, though: How much did the school really win? If you ask me, this strict adherence to "Policy" was penny-wise, pound-foolish. Granted, the school's sole owner is a millionaire. Her three locations allow her to spend the entire summer (her school's busiest time of the year) on Martha's Vineyard without once leaving the island. Maybe she's content with the state of her business, and doesn't feel the need to change a thing.

But ...wow, that's some terrible karma. Her students know when they're being ripped off. They resent it. They tell friends at home, and at other schools in Boston. I'm sure she's lost relationships with some of the foreign travel agents who together bring her eighty percent of her students. Over time, this kind of practice can ruin a company's reputation, and with it, its business.

The worst part of all this is that these students don't speak enough English to win an argument in our language. Imagine the disadvantage! They are alone in a new country, unsure of its laws and customs. Most become indignant, but others shrug and think, "Policy? What can you do, then? Oh, well," because that's how it works in their cultures.

But it doesn't work that way in American culture!

When you go to a store, how do you feel when you see a sign that reads, "No Exchange, No Return" or "No Refunds?" It makes you hesitant to buy, doesn't it? How does that help the business to profit? It scares sales away.

Restocking fees? They're simply gouging you. Who puts up with that?

Here's my favorite: you deposit cash via the ATM one night, and the next day a check is presented that you did not have funds for – until you made that deposit! But, despite an envelope full of dough in their "in" box, you get charged $25 or $35 for …what? The pleasure of banking with them?

A close favorite in my disservice hit parade: your credit card has a $10,000 limit. You're close to maxed out, but you've lost track of how much you've spent. At no time does your card get declined, but then in the mail, miraculously, your statement tells you you're in big trouble because you've exceeded your limit by $200. Penalties are severe, and you're in danger of losing your card privileges as well! Granted, as an adult it's your responsibility to keep track of your finances, but even adults are only human. And besides, your card was never declined! Isn't it reasonable to expect the credit card company to monitor your balance, and decline your purchase so that you *don't* go over?

Yes, if you've guessed that I've fallen victim to these indignities myself, you're correct. I refuse to pay the penalties, though. I'll (calmly and politely) put up any amount of stink, demand to speak to supervisors and their supervisors, until I get my account credited the amount of the "service" charges.

…And that's the point! People, real people, make all policies in the world. You can't argue with gravity, but you can lobby your town government to change a speed limit, and you can sometimes talk yourself out of a speeding ticket, too.

People decide when checks are cut. People decide whether or not your surgery will be paid for by your insurance. People set the policy that allows customer service professionals to take care of problems themselves, or the policy that forces them to say, "I'm sorry, but there's nothing I can do. That's policy."

Policies, rules, even laws, have their place. They're the little white lines that tell us where to drive, so we don't go into the oncoming traffic. They give us guidance when two conflicting parties both want it their way. But policies have their limits, too.

Five-star customer service follows policies, but only as guidelines. As a professional, you have to be ready to explain the policy as well as the reasoning behind it. You also have to be willing and able to circumvent policy to make your customer happy.

If you're a business owner or executive, your job is to set policy, to write the rules of the game that is your business. But if you don't enable your customer service reps to bend the rules in order to satisfy a customer, yours will never be a five-star organization.

Your customers know that policies are set by people, and that people can overrule policy. If you don't do it, the customer is going to take his business to your competitor.

Discussion Questions

1. How much latitude are you given to bend the rules?

2. How often do you do it?

3. How many times in the past week have you said something like, "It's policy," to your customers? In the last month?

4. What other phrases can you think of that are similar in spirit to "It's policy?"

6

YOUR INTERNAL CUSTOMERS

"Good actions give strength to ourselves and
inspire good actions in others."
Plato

About the time I went off to college, my father partnered
up on a groundbreaking study with a Ph.D. psychologist
specializing in organizational development.

For his entire career, my father gave career advice to top
executives at some of the world's most successful companies,
including Digital Computers, AT&T, and Wang (this was
some time ago, when all three were giants in their fields).
He worked with venture capitalists to recruit presidents
and other top brass to start-ups in the biotech industry. In
short, my father knew the traits of a leader better than any
man I know, and he put his knowledge to work with his
colleague.

Their study was on the personality types of *change agents*, whom they ended up calling Total Quality Leaders.

While the Total Quality Management (TQM) movement pretty much fizzled out right as my father retired in the early '90s, the lessons he taught me from TQM have stuck with me ever since. The good news is, while TQM as a term has fallen out of favor in corporate America, many of its key points have been incorporated into mainstream business practices (in Six Sigma, among other things).

Perhaps you're thinking, "Good for Ted's Dad. So what?" Fair enough. Let me explain how the principles of TQM pertain to your job, and to this chapter.

Central to TQM was the belief that companies have internal as well as external customers. Sure, the buyer working for another company, or the consumer, has to be treated well or they'll take their business to the next guy. That's why we're here, isn't it? Absolutely.

But an internal customer…. What's that?

Discussion Questions

1. What is an internal customer?

2. What makes these people customers? Doesn't a customer have to pay the company money, and buy something?

Stop! Do Not Turn the page until you have answered these questions.

Your coworkers are your internal customers.

Treat them appropriately.

How is that, you say? Again, your coworkers aren't spending money on company product; how can they be customers?

Try again. If all of you in your company do not start thinking of each other as customers, and acting accordingly, you are never going to achieve your five-star potential. Indeed, no matter how good you *personally* are at delivering excellent service, if you and those you work with don't adopt this thinking, there is no way your company's "machine" will run smoothly enough for your top-tier service standards to ever be met.

Cooperation throughout your company, based on mutual respect and total commitment to its goals, is the only way to achieve five-star customer service.

What are customers? They are strangers who we want to become close friends. The thing is that friends, unlike family, can always break off relations if you don't treat them right. So you have to remain nice to your friends at all times, or risk losing them.

Whether you work for a large company or small, the rules still apply. Say your job is to take customers' orders over the phone. To do this, you have to interact with the warehouse and with shipping all day long in order to get your customers' orders flowing efficiently. You have to be friendly to your coworkers in the back of the house. You have to treat them with respect, even if you've been to college and they haven't, or yours is a white-collar job and they get dirty at work; even if you get paid more than they do or, conversely, even if you're unhappy because they get paid more than you!

In order to serve your external customers better, you have to listen to these internal customers when they complain about the demands you put on them. Together, you have to work out ways that you can address their gripes while still accomplishing what you need to get done. Working together effectively, communicating and brainstorming as a team, you'll do infinitely better than if you just go on as usual, with everyone mad at each other.

Of course, these others have to treat you well, too. You're each other's customers. It's a two-way street. And they should realize that their jobs will become much easier – and their evaluations better – if they can work more smoothly with you.

Perhaps, since you are reading this book and they are probably not, you should step up and make the first move. Take the initiative to make a change.

As one of your firm's customer service professionals, it is up to you to initiate and maintain a culture of respect and cooperation that your coworkers will adopt and develop. Like it or not, you're a leader now.

Is the dynamic of the internal customer beginning to make some sense now? Let's try another example, just to make sure.

This is one from the service industry that I've seen too many times: Often waiters are treated like third-class citizens in their restaurants. It is quite typical for cooks, and even more so chefs, to verbally abuse waiters – even to yell at them, and sometimes to reduce them to tears. Bartenders sometimes do it, and managers have been known to participate as well.

Discussion Questions

1. Why do you think waiters are singled out for such bad treatment?

2. How could that adversely affect the smooth functioning of the establishment?

3. How could this practice impede quality customer service?

I can only give you theories for the first question. Right now, I'd like to move on to the second.

Waiters are a restaurant's front-line workers. They are the company's customer service professionals. It is the waiter who represents the entire company to the guest. Often, the guest interacts with no one else throughout the meal.

If the management has its act together (and sadly, that's not common in this field), this kind of behavior won't be tolerated. The chef, the bartender, and the manager are all there to help the wait staff do its job well. They really should treat waiters and waitresses like internal customers, and give them the support service they need.

But it goes the other way, too. I've worked in a number of restaurants, and I know what goes on in functional and dysfunctional ones alike. There are plenty of waiters who work the system for their own benefit: who zip into the kitchen or to the service bar with special orders, expecting their coworkers to drop everything to help them with their particular issues. Sometimes a waiter will accept help from other waiters – running food out to his tables, clearing his tables, etc. – and will not reciprocate.

That's not okay, either. If everyone in a restaurant is an internal customer, then everyone will help everyone without being asked, and the whole operation will begin to hum. Without this type of cooperation, exemplary customer service will elude the entire organization.

Discussion Questions:

1. Chances are you don't work in a restaurant. So how can that last example help you?

2. There is also a chance that your position in your company is not technically in customer service at all. How can you take the lesson of this chapter and make it work for you?

3. What if you "get it," but nobody else in your company has read this book – or even would, if you left it lying on their desk with a ribbon on it! What if your company is suffering from the all-too-common malaise of "My department (or even just of "Me") versus Them?" Is this chapter simply too pie-in-the-sky to help you? Or is there something you can do on your own initiative that could make a difference?

4. What would your boss say if you gave him this book? What would the Big Boss of your company (owner, president, CEO, etc.) say if you gave *her* a copy of this book?

From The Trenches:

Do It Right and
Your Customers Won't Be Tempted to Leave

My friends at Roche Bros. have quite a number of events every year, two of the biggest being their Service Awards for associates, and a gala Vendor Recognition party for firms like mine. (While I personally think we vendors should be the ones hosting a party for *them*, I haven't shared this opinion with the company brass yet.) In recent years these two parties have been consistently held at the Newton Marriott. Sure, this hotel enjoys a central location to their stores and main office, but so do several dozen others. Why, I asked, does this Marriott win their business year after year?

Customer service. (Surprised?) I don't think it's giving away a big secret to say, Marriott banquet fare is pretty good, but it's not five-star cuisine. The hotel lobby and ballrooms are also very nice, but they don't compare to the Park Plaza. Still, Roche Bros. executives, customer service gurus all, are highly impressed with Marriott's attentiveness.

As one Roche Bros.' executive told me, "They always – *always* – anticipate our needs. Their sales manager understands our budget, and never tries to gouge us. In fact, it's gotten to the point where we just tell him how many people and what kind of event it is, and he puts it all together for us to approve. Turn-around is typically only a day.

"The hors d'oeuvres and meals he recommends are perfect for us. The events are always sufficiently staffed, so no one ever waits for anything. The staff is sharp and really courteous: we've never had to complain, not once. They do a top job from start to finish."

Asked if they were likely to try another hotel anytime soon, this executive replied a quick "Why would we? As with our ESL classes, we've tried other vendors. We're approached all the time by competitors looking for our patronage. But we're completely satisfied. Why take the risk, or subject ourselves to the hassle, or to the embarrassment? Could you imagine what the Roches would say if they hosted a party with bad service? They'd look bad in front of their guests, and whoever chose that hotel would look bad in front of them. As long as that hotel keeps its performance this sharp, it'll keep our business."

Discussion Questions

1. Go back and find three things the Newton Marriott does to distinguish itself in Boston's competitive banquet market.

2. Why do they bother with these extra touches?

3. What one thing do you think impresses Roche Bros. the most? Keep in mind how precious time is for executives these days.

4. How can you apply some of the lessons of the Newton Marriott to your job? List five things you could do in your work that the Marriott's manager might try if you traded jobs for a week.

7

SELLING THE
FIVE-STAR WAY

"The most important persuasion tool you
have in your entire arsenal is integrity."
- Zig Ziglar

This is not a sales book. While I know a thing or two about
that field, that's not what this book is about.

However, sales and customer service are inextricably linked:
if your organization sells in a way that is inconsistent with the
standards of five-star customer service, the rest of the staff
will find it difficult, if not impossible, to rise to the five-star
level in their areas of responsibility.

How a company sells is one very important aspect of its
standard of customer service. While this chapter does not
cover every aspect of how sales and customer service overlap,
I think it will be helpful to discuss some of the highlights
of the relationship between how a firm's customers are sold
to and how those customers judge their experience and the

quality of the organization. The bid for a customer's loyalty is often either won or lost in their sales experience.

Don't abuse your customers' trust

The following two stories cover almost identical situations, but they were handled much differently. See what you can learn from them.

Every year we hold our Christmas party in a restaurant, and it's inevitably a good time. We try to feed our colleagues well. Drinks flow, laughs abound; teachers are by nature extroverts, and at our party we all let our hair down for a night of mild debauchery. I'll bet we're not the only company that does this.

One year not long ago, when our waitress presented us with the check, she failed to point out that an eighteen percent tip had already been added. Now granted, as a veteran waiter and bartender, I should have expected it: adding a tip to parties of six or more is pretty standard in the food service field. But I'd had more than my share of champagne, and ...well, I wasn't thinking, pure and simple.

I'm a generous tipper anyway, and we'd had a great time, so I looked at the big, circled number at the bottom of the bill and added something over twenty percent for the tip. The only thing was that I was tipping twenty percent-plus *in addition to* eighteen percent. In fact, I was including the eighteen percent tip in my calculation for the second tip!

I'm too embarrassed to name the sum. Suffice it to say, the next day I felt badly burned. Was the waitress obligated to bring the automatic charge to my attention? Not technically. But, in gouging me through this sin of omission, she turned me off to her restaurant. I haven't gone back since. I wonder how many other customers this has happened to, and what they did in response.

Compare that to the story of the waiter who served us lunch one day at Legal Sea Foods. It was an important meeting, one in which my company formed a strategic partnership with a prestigious university. Sure, I was inclined to feel warmly toward the waiter who'd been part of this auspicious meeting. But then he went above and beyond, and showed me anew why people line up to frequent this particular chain.

Our waiter, Phil, did something I really appreciated: our bill was $99, and I gave him two fifty-dollar certificates plus my credit card. Rather than just ringing up some random fee on my card, he brought it back and pointed out that we owed nothing on our bill.

Of course, the credit card was for his tip. But the fact that he didn't presume so really impressed me. When I explained what it was for, he only sought pre-authorization for one penny on the card, which again was not presuming anything. (I tipped him a bit more than that.)

It's just a bad idea to take advantage of your customers. Treat them honorably. Usually, they will prove that they deserve that trust. If they don't? You'll have to write the experience off as a loss on your taxes. As a five-star customer service professional – and I stress the word *professional* – you really don't have a choice in the matter.

…Which is not to say that you should let people abuse your trust. If you own a retail establishment, you have no choice but to protect yourself from shoplifters. If you catch them, by all means, send them to jail, and do it publicly. If a client refuses to pay you for services rendered, you may have to end up suing them; at the very least, don't do business with this company again. We all get burned from time to time, and it isn't feasible to go through life pretending we don't. You certainly won't stay in business that way.

Discussion Questions

1. How are the two restaurant situations the same?

2. How are they different?

3. What ramifications did these waiters' actions have on their restaurants?

4. What do you think, personally, about each waiter?

5. What would you have done in each situation?

6. What lesson can you take from this example to your own job?

Know your field better than your competitors, and share that knowledge with your clients.

I may be nice, a touchy-feely teacher who likes to garden and play with his daughters and all, but I am also fiercely competitive. When it comes to my business, I don't wish poor fortune to my competitors – I just want to challenge them to raise their standard of play a bit. And if I swipe some of their clients along the way, well, they should remember one important rule: treat your customers right, and they'll never stray.

The way that I appropriate a competitor's clients is through superior customer service at least as much as superior product. When I speak to a competitor's client about the programs they have in place, I ask a few pointed questions: for instance, do they know their training is tax-deductible as a necessary business expense? If they're in Massachusetts, are they aware of the state fund that can pay for their training program? There are plenty more, but these two often get me an appointment, and from there I will usually win the company's business.

To me, this type of customer service is a given: in order to sell my best, I have to know all there is to know about my field that may benefit the customer. I have to share that information. If they need more details, I have to be ready to provide it for them.

Know your field: you owe it to your customer. That alone can make you wildly successful.

Discussion Questions

1. How well do you know your field, and every related detail that can be of use to your customer?

2. How well do your competitors know your field?

3. How clearly do your customers and prospects appreciate your expertise in your field, and how your knowledge can benefit them?

Never, *ever* force a sale.

There are two mutually exclusive philosophies in sales. The first says, "Get the sale and run." (Think of the movie *Glen Gary, Glen Ross*. Missed it? Think of a used car salesman.) The second school of thought says, "Build a long-term relationship. Foster the goodwill of your customers, and residual sales will raise your company to great heights."

You can't differentiate sales from customer service: each serve – or cripples – the other. So if you intend to build a reputation for yourself and your company as paragons of customer service, please, don't 'use' your customers, and don't allow your sales staff to, either. A quick hit now through an unethical, forced sale, will hurt you many-fold with that customer and all others as well.

Discussion Questions

1. Does your sales process serve or take advantage of your customers?

2. No, really.

Give Your Customers What *They* Want, Not What *You* Want

Did I say sales and customer service were intimately related? The two are also conjoined with product.

"How's that?" You ask. If you're selling in an obnoxious or irresponsible way, you're abusing your customers, and that's terrible customer service. Similarly, if you're trying to pawn off something they don't want, don't need, or that just isn't all that good – if the sale doesn't benefit the customer more than it does your company - then again, you're not taking their best interests to heart; that's not serving your customers, is it?

Back in my twenties I worked for three different companies selling three very different types of products. What tied them together for me was that I believed, at least initially, in each product. What later drove me to leave each company was that my interaction with customers and prospects taught me that the companies I represented were not offering what the customers really wanted. In each case, they were good ideas with good after-the-sale service to back them up, but in not being responsive to the desires of the market, the companies in question were giving bad customer service. And since I was making the sales (and usually doing a fine job of it, too) I increasingly felt dishonest, and had to move on.

I was perhaps most excited about the third company. Its product, water sub-metering for entire apartment communities, was immensely profitable to the customer (the property owner), helped tenants by keeping their rents stable, and it beneficial to the environment, as it encouraged conservation by the tenants. There was only one problem: the landlords I spoke to wanted a low-cost, no-frills product, and the company I worked for only wanted to sell an expensive product rife with (profitable) bells and whistles. Basically, we were trying to sell Mercedes to people in the market for a Hyundai.

I told my employer what my prospects said, but to no avail. When it got to the point that my disillusion impeded my sales efforts and made it hard for me to sleep at night, I left that company as I had the two previous.

Eventually, this string of negative experiences drove me from sales; it was only when I was able to create my own product that I was attracted to selling again. And guess what? I love it! I love what I sell because it is *exactly* what my customers want. How can I be so sure? Because I ask them what they want, then give it to them – plus a whole lot more than they'd ever hope to expect, of course, because I'm a professional.

It stuns me that most companies don't do this. Cable TV companies bundle channels together into packages, rather than allowing consumers to choose à la carte. I can't imagine how that serves the customer or the provider, I really can't. Cell phone companies make you guess how many minutes you're going to use beforehand. That's got to be one of the most perverse setups I've ever heard of. It's as if the entire industry were inspired by a Monty Python skit.

Conversely, iTunes allows you to buy as many or as few songs as you like, when you like; Netflix charges you one low price to watch as many or as few movies a month as you desire. Both business models give the consumer exactly what she wants, and that means that each gives superior customer service via the product that it sells.

Discussion Questions

1. Name five more industries in which the product itself exemplifies bad customer service.

2. How could a company in one of those industries clean up its act?

3. Would that reform bring the company in question more business and more profits, or just more headache?

Never say *No*

A big part of what my company does is cater to the needs of our client corporations. That means, in effect, that we try never to say "No." Personally, I feel allergic to that word.

That's not to say that clients don't ever ask us for things that we can't give them. Some requests simply won't work. For instance, if a client wants an ESL course taught by a bilingual teacher who will explain things in students' native language, we simply won't do it. We conduct our ESL classes entirely in English, and there's very solid pedagogy behind it. If a student translates, he'll never attain fluency, no matter how hard he tries.

Now, my point isn't teaching theory; it's customer service. Specifically, find a way not to say *No*. And in the case I just illustrated, I cannot say *Yes*.

Here's what I do instead: When I can't say *Yes*, I explain why not. Often that will completely satisfy my client. After all, I'm the expert in my field. Clients come up with requests and suggestions because they have good ideas. It's just that those good ideas aren't always applicable.

Another example is when a client wants a class with fifteen students. I explain that while we can do it, the pace of the class will slow dramatically. We won't guarantee our results. When they pay for a 48-hour session, they are also paying for one level of progress. This won't happen with fifteen students. If the client insists, I explain that there's a charge for every student after eight. The class of fifteen will be the same price as two classes of eight and seven, and with two classes they'll get the results we guarantee for a small class. When I explain it this way, clients invariably take my advice.

That last point illustrates my second rule of thumb, namely, I suggest an attractive alternative. Someone wants *This*, I offer him *That* instead, and show him why *This* isn't nearly as suitable for his company as *That*.

Notice that in all this discussion, I've never said *No. No* doesn't help anyone. Rather, it sets up an adversarial condition that hinders compromise.

Of course, there are situations in this world where *No* isn't just helpful, it's necessary. If a prospective client insists on classes at half-price, that's an easy *No* for me. But they weren't serious in the first place. If I can show them how our prices are getting them much more than another provider who charges so much less, they'll almost always – actually, to date, they *always* – acquiesce.

Step One:
Explain Why Not

Step Two:
Suggest an Attractive Alternative

You don't have to take it from me, though. Remember that lunch at Legal Sea Foods with Phil the waiter, who was so gracious about his tip? Phil impressed me in another way as well.

Phil wanted to sell us dessert, but my guest, Julie, only had interest in one thing: dark chocolate. She asked Phil if he had any on the menu, and Phil replied, "How about I bring a plate of six bonbons? They're delicious!"

Julie said, "Are they dark chocolate?" It was clear from her tone that she knew the answer. Phil's answer was a prime example of the conversational judo I recommend:

"I know what you'll like! We have a deep, rich flourless chocolate cake. It's hot from the oven, and it's got chocolate fudge sauce sprinkled all over the top. You're gonna die."

We snapped it up right away. Julie hadn't been fooled; she knew the dessert Phil sold us was made with milk chocolate. But it was such a delicious-sounding alternative, she couldn't resist. And I'm not sure about Julie, but every meal *I* eat at Legal is now topped off with this irresistible dessert.

Phil hadn't said *No* to us. That would have ended the conversation, and our dessert order as well. He couldn't explain *why* the menu had no dark chocolate; what reason is there? A restaurant can't offer everything in creation, that's all. So instead, Phil moved right on to Step Two and suggested an attractive alternative. He got our bill (and his tip) higher, so he won. Legal got our bill up, so they won. And we had one of the best desserts on the face of the earth, so we were more than happy. For that reason we'll all definitely go back, and we'll all win again …and again …and again.

Phil's verbal judo, his countering an unfillable request with an attractive alternative, made winners of us all. We spent more, but we were happy that we did! Phil definitely gave us five-star customer service.

Discussion Questions

1. What is wrong with saying *No*? What happens, psychologically, when you say *No* to a customer?

2. What are the two methods you can try when you want to avoid saying *No* to a customer?

3. When do you find yourself saying *No* (or *I'm sorry*, or *We can't…*) to a customer now?

4. How will you, your company, and your customer all benefit if you master this lesson and remove *No* from your workplace vocabulary?

In The Eyes of Your Customer, "Free" Is Worth Every Penny

Gadzooks! Sometimes you can be too accommodating to a customer, and when you are, no one prospers.

My own example of this comes from a situation in which I didn't even sell; I *gave* three months of classes away *for free!*

Now generally, I'm suspicious of the word Free. I look at the whole Internet ethic of "Free Everything" with disdain. It's nice and all, but …somehow un-American. If you're going to donate your time, do it at a homeless shelter. Don't give away what someone else would gladly charge money for.

So why did I do it? I gave one class away because I was overconfident. Basically, I was so sure the client, my first Fortune 500 company, would be impressed and order more classes (for pay the next time) that I took a gamble.

This was at the start of my corporate ESL venture. I was deep in the middle of a long and very rewarding relationship with

Roche Bros., and had a few other highly satisfied clients as well. Things were going so well for all concerned that I *knew* I had a winner – such a winner that I was sure, "to know me is to love me." I also had a great relationship with the HR manager at the distribution site where I'd be teaching – she was taking Spanish at our school in Stoughton – and I was referred by one of this company's vice presidents. How could I lose?

Here's how: the site manager counted pennies, but had no idea about dollars. When we met, he was amazed that I mentioned reduction in turnover as one of our courses' benefits to the employer. "Turnover!" he said to his HR partner. "How did he know that's our biggest problem at this facility?"

It's *everyone's* biggest problem before we go in, that's how. But this guy – so proud of himself for saving 25 cents per unit ("That's $250,000 per day!") – had no idea that his human workers were his most important resources, and he wasn't managing them well – or, to put it in terms this self-professed "numbers guy" might better understand, he wasn't utilizing these resources to their full potential, and so his facility was hemorrhaging money. If a 25-cent mistake could cost his company so much money when factored over the course of a day, how much did absenteeism, workman's comp, recruitment and training, sluggish productivity due to poor morale, and other human issues cost him? A lot more than a quarter-million dollars, for sure!

Sooner rather than later, this guy was let go, and replaced by a dynamic, talented manager who saw the value of morale in his operation, and who opted to offer ESL as a benefit – a very well received benefit, for that matter. As usual, he tried us out with one class, and was so impressed with the results he got that he ordered three classes for the following session.

But that was later. My original class for the first manager was a failure almost from day one. Without the site manager's support, a couple of the lead workers harassed their subordinates into avoiding class – one even followed his guy to our classroom to check up on him. Sharp, morale-building move.

Others dropped out for various reasons, including one injury and one termination. I graduated only one student of eight at the end of our three-month course. And long before that, the site manager's ambivalence to the program convinced me that there would be no more classes on his watch.

Oh, well. As I remind myself daily, "Fail Forward." I learned from the experience; that lesson, though frustrating, was worth my time. Now I'm sharing it with you, so you don't have to live through the same.

The bottom line is that this guy did not want to buy from me. Giving him for free what he had no interest in buying was a mistake. I should have walked away, and spent those classroom hours selling to someone who wanted our classes. (As it turns out, to the delight of my wife, children, and mortgage company, there's a world full of such enlightened managers.)

Discussion Questions

1. Have you ever sold to someone who just didn't want or need (or see the need for) your product or service?

2. Customer service, when done right, often involves inside sales to existing customers. Are you under pressure to "upsell" things that you know are not in your customers' best interests?

3. Long-term, what do you think happens to your company in cases like that? Does it benefit or suffer from such sales techniques?

4. Have you ever successfully sold to someone who doesn't want your product, only to find her grateful for the experience? (Actually, this can work out, though I'd say rarely in my experience.)

Don't Stalk Your Clients

For the first few years of my business I had uncannily bad luck with technical people (accountants and web site designers, in particular), so much in fact that I have to admit, the problem probably lay more with me and my inability to relate to them than it did with that entire portion of the population.

Having said that, I can't take all of the blame for this one.

Early in my business I met an accountant at my local chamber of commerce. I was still pretty small-time, and I'd just had to dump our last accountant (a relative) for inattentiveness. I knew this new gentleman from a chamber group we both participated in; he was respected by the other members, so I figured I'd give him a try.

From the beginning, things could have gone better. For one thing, he was an accountant who specialized in serving small businesses and helping guide their growth, yet his own firm was really just he and some seasonal part-time help. In other words, he didn't practice what he preached. If that doesn't make you apprehensive, perhaps it should. Why hadn't his firm grown, even a little?

Another incongruity related to his specialty was that he never, ever wore a jacket or tie. I'm sorry if I come across as conservative, but when you work as a consultant for other companies, you have to dress the part of a professional and an expert. And if you're an accountant, lawyer, or banker... those are three of the stodgiest professions there are. I think our society has a uniform for these three fields that includes single-breasted suits and really boring ties. Certainly that's the case in the Northeast.

Those are two surface complaints, and I was willing to be open-minded and overlook them. Hiring this character involved an omen I might have paid more attention to, though.

I rang the accountant (let's call him Frank) to ask him to help us with our taxes. He insisted on meeting with Jane and me. Interesting, as he'd just made the sale, but it was his trip, so why not?

Frank came to our house and tried to pressure-close us... although we had already delivered ourselves as a neatly wrapped present at his feet. He used sales techniques that I'd picked up a week into my first sales job – and that I'd outgrown by week four. Jane and I thought it was obnoxious and/or comical. Jane didn't like Frank. She wanted to look elsewhere, but (fool that I was) I stuck by him. I've learned better than to second-guess her since then.

He did our taxes just fine, and the following year he did as well. We ended up getting refunds both years, a quite sizable one the second year, in fact. We had absolutely no complaints with his work. Furthermore, Frank came at a reasonable price.

Had he behaved more professionally, Frank would still be our accountant today.

Sadly, Frank began to stalk us. I say this in jest – there was never a need for a restraining order – but the fact of the matter is that Frank stopped treating us like his clients, and started demanding our attention. You can't demand *anything* of your customers. It doesn't work that way.

I have to admit another weakness: for several years, I did not treat outsiders working for me as well as I treat my clients and coworkers. Since then, I've mended my ways for reasons of courtesy. But at the time, when I was someone else's client, I often used to give that person very little of my attention – not from inherent rudeness, just because I was busy trying to serve *my* clients well. Frank wanted me to return his numerous calls promptly, and I rarely returned them at all. While that may have made it harder for him to help me, I figured, "Hey, that's my problem, not his. After all, I'm the one who needs his help. If I pass on it, that's my loss, right?"

Frank didn't see it that way. He began to lecture me whenever he did manage to reach me. Naturally, that just made getting me all the harder, as I was now not just too busy to speak with him, but reluctant to as well. Finally exasperated, he sent me a letter, not unlike a boy who has been mistreated by his girlfriend. Yikes! Not only was it plaintive and colossally unprofessional, his writing skills were atrocious! (Never send a poorly written letter to an English teacher).

Okay, that last comment was made tongue-in-cheek. The issue that got Frank replaced, though, was that he'd written that letter at all. Frank forgot who was the customer and who the customer service provider. He lost sight of the fact that, no matter how badly your customer treats you, you cannot correct his behavior. The best you can do for yourself, as a five-star customer service professional, is put up with it or fire your customer.

Discussion Questions

1. What were the things that Frank did right?

2. What were the things that he did wrong?

3. Do you agree with me that a customer service professional can never correct his customer?

4. Have you ever had a difficult customer to work with? Not one who is too demanding, but rather, one who does not keep enough contact for you to help him as well as you'd like to? What did you do?

5. What could you do, without correcting him, to get this type of customer to pay more attention to you?

6. What other option do you always have in a situation such as this?

I know exactly how Frank felt dealing with me because, at the same time that I was ignoring him, I had to suffer a client that ignored me.

It was my very first corporate client, a small manufacturer down in Plymouth with twenty ESL students to train. I grossly undercharged this employer, but was still happy for the experience. However, it was not the ideal situation that most of our corporate clients have provided us since. Actually, I'm glad I got it out of the way so I could move on to greener pastures.

This company gave me twenty students divided into two classes of ten each. As is often the case, my contact was the human resources manager. That's usually a good thing. But this manager was …difficult to work with, let's say.

She wasn't difficult because she was demanding. Au contraire, I was looking forward to a challenge, so I could show off my stuff. I asked her for work-related materials to help me custom design the course. A week passed, then another, and I received nothing. Students stopped coming to class. I tried to call. Nothing. I left her notes. No reply.

I worked at this facility for three months, and I only heard from her twice. I had no access to her office. She never returned my calls or replied to my emails. It was disappointing and frustrating. I knew there was so much more that I could give this company, if only somebody *cared!*

Still, we got some great results. The story with the missing students, it turned out, was that there had been a layoff.

My remaining students let me know this once they had enough English under their belts to express themselves. These survivors did a great job – despite abysmal literacy across the board, all improved at least one level by the end of the session.

How did I get my customer to pay me the attention that I desired? I didn't. I let my contact know that I wanted to speak with her, and about what. That was all I could do. She didn't give me any feedback at all about the course, and didn't respond to my query about continuing the program, either. But I got paid for my work, did it exceptionally well, and ...well, as that was all she wanted, that was that.

I'm not a bit surprised that this poorly managed company had to lay off a large number of its workers. But that's for another book.

I moved on to bigger and better projects. Then one day, a strategic partner called with a hot lead: it turned out to be this company!

I'm not one to turn away business, so I called her. I got her voice mail and left her a message. That was five months ago. I still haven't heard a word. I do know one thing, though: that company remains without an ESL provider.

Sometimes you just have to chalk one up to experience.

Discussion Questions

1. Do you have vendors or contractors whom you are currently neglecting?

1. Is it possible that you could benefit in some way if you had closer communications with them?

2. Do you agree that there is ultimately nothing a customer service provider can do to impel his customer to keep in better contact? If no, what can the provider do?

Do for your customer what no one else can

We won a $50,000 contract with a small manufacturer one time because we were the only company that was responsive enough for their needs. This firm was rushing to get their state grant proposal in, and had only three days left. The grant writer knew us, and was well aware of how aggressive we are in winning sales. He called us, we met with the manufacturer first thing the next morning, and our part of the grant was done, after many revisions, within thirty-six hours.

For $50,000, I think most people would be happy to lose a few hours of sleep. But it turns out, our contact the grant writer knew that of all of the companies in our field, we were the only ones who would hustle for that contract.

I have to shake my head when I think of it. That type of turnaround should be a given in any company. But it's not, not even remotely. Without us, the client would have had to forgo a vital part of its training. We filled a need, and no one else was willing to bother. That's what makes such responsiveness five-star.

Discussion Questions

1. What would you do for an additional $50,000 this year?

2. All right, that money isn't all for you. It's actually your company's revenue, and perhaps you won't even see a commission from it. My question remains: what would you do to win your company that business?

3. Does everyone in your company share this ethic? What would the rest of your colleagues do if a similar, last-minute situation like this came up? (If your company is larger, just keep adding zeros until the figure begins to impress you.)

From The Trenches:

Five-Star Service Upstairs;
Ball Dropped Downstairs

For Jane's birthday this year, I rented a room at a new Boston hotel, Jury's. From the valet on, this well-established Irish chain really impressed us. Everyone was so polite, friendly, and helpful, and there was so much staff on hand, that we felt we were getting five-star service in what otherwise is probably a four-star hotel: a perfect story for this book.

Ah, if only the bar staff had the customer service training of their coworkers upstairs.

We'd chosen that particular hotel because a close friend had heard great things about the bar; it was one of Boston's "In" places for the summer Newport crowd, from which we'd graduated a few years before. As we wanted to catch up with our friends, it was a perfect venue for a birthday party.

Don't misunderstand me; we had a great time. But I'm never off duty as a customer service teacher, and the atrocity that was the bar service killed me.

The bartenders were too slow. It was as if it were an open bar, paid for by the hotel, and they had strict instructions to pour as few drinks as possible. They had also been meticulously trained in how to go an entire shift without breaking one smile. To compound these issues, the bar was grossly understaffed.

If you're going to be criminally slothful, at least be nice about it!

I've been there: bartender to my social peers, some of whom are a bit self-impressed and treat me like "the help." There's some of that with the Newport crowd. It takes an emotional toll to be looked down on so, in an egalitarian society such as ours.

But bar patrons – especially lavish tippers and professional partiers like our friends – can also be a blast to work with. Just imagine: all of these happy people out celebrating the end of a long week, flirting with you, having a blast in part because of the excellent service you provide… and you're making money from it! Speed up and smile, and the money flows like the drinks you serve. You can't beat it with a stick (though I can't imagine why you'd want to).

I'm not writing this to encourage you to change careers and break into bartending. It gets old soon enough. All I'm saying is, your attitude is going to shape your entire experience at work. If you're miserable by nature or inclination, you'll have a terrible time – and you'll give terrible service.

If your staff is miserable …cut your losses. There's a world *full* of talented and friendly bartenders, as well as bank tellers, call-center operators, plant managers, and anything else, for that matter. Recruiting the best is no big deal. It's worth the extra effort.

Discussion Questions

1. Whose fault is the poor service in this bar? The bartenders? The patrons? The manager?

2. What can the manager do to change the ethic in this bar?

3. Are the bartenders beyond saving? What could be done to win them away from their abominable customer service?

4. Can the guests be changed? After all, some of them are a bit snooty. Others probably don't tip properly. Maybe that's why the staff is so dispirited.

5. How does the poor customer service in the bar reflect on the rest of the hotel? What if the bar isn't actually run by the hotel, but leased to an outside operation? What bearing does that have on the guests' perception of the hotel?

6. What would you do as (a) the hotel manager, (b) the bar manager, (c) a bartender, (d) a bar patron?

8

CUSTOMER SERVICE: EXPENSE? ...OR INVESTMENT?

"Penny wise, pound foolish."
- Benjamin Franklin

You can't escape this fact: customer service increases payroll. Go to the Waldorf Astoria Hotel and you'll never wait for valet parking or a bellhop; the desk will have a clerk ready for you... it's amazing. And really, really expensive. Compare that to Motel Six: one clerk, often on the other side of a bulletproof glass partition. Not expensive at all.

As I mentioned earlier in this book, Roche Bros. Supermarkets spends *twice* as much on payroll as it's biggest competitor. Twice as much! Every day of their lives, the top brass at Roche Bros. has to make the decision to keep their high standards – and high spending – up. They have to say to themselves, What if we just shave off one job here, one there? Would it hurt us so badly? We're growing; we wouldn't even have to lay off, just transfer.

Maybe they could save some money and not suffer adverse consequences if they dropped their staff by five percent. Maybe they could get away with ten. Maybe several fewer full-time spots in each store would make a big difference on their bottom line.

But at some point – some as yet *unknown* point – their impeccable standards would suffer. Then they'd just be another grocery store. My guess is, their competitor, with its hundreds of stores and countless millions of dollars to spend on advertising, would put them out of business in short order. Customer service, even more than superior meat and produce, is what defines this company. It's why people shop there. It's what keeps their checkout line humming all day long, even when their competitor's stores are slow.

When you take pride out of the picture and just look at the numbers of the situation (which is something publicly owned companies *have* to do), the temptation is always there to reduce customer service and save a few bucks.

Executives have to make a simple but crucial decision every time they think about the topic of customer service, and that is, Can we afford it?

Maybe, maybe not. Let's explore this question a bit more.

In a perfect world, everyone would have the pride in their company to make customer service their top priority. But this world isn't perfect, and there's a little issue that often gets in the way of perfection, called budget. If your company operates on 5% margin, and training and employing sufficient staff would increase your expenses by 10% ...it's just not feasible. At least, not unless you can increase your market share dramatically, and make a smaller take on a much larger customer base. This is how Roche Bros., Legal Sea Foods, Lifeline, Stew Leonard's, and many others do it, but it may not work for every company in every industry.

The thing is, there is a plethora of fields where there is no competition in customer service at all. Take your electric company as an example. Since my childhood in the eighties, I've been hearing about deregulation fostering competition, but it doesn't ring true in the case of utilities for the simple reason that, if I want to go with another electricity provider, I'm out of luck. If I stay with gas, I'm stuck with my gas company. Or take cell phone service. Boston has at least five big companies to choose from, maybe more. But no one's competing on customer service. For years, I actually chose my provider because of its reputation for serving the business community so well. Then my phone needed repair, and I was sent to stand in a *three-hour* line at some far-away location with surly clerks. I sized up the situation and left, choosing instead to pay a premium (and wait days with no cell phone) for their mail-in repair option. My entire company now does business with another carrier.

I'm sorry to say this – I feel like a blasphemer – but none of these industries have any compelling reason to provide customer service. Until some outside market force gives them reason, it's simply not important to the decision-makers in these companies. I suppose it shouldn't be, either.

...Or should it? I'm not so sure that cell phone companies, at least, couldn't benefit from improved customer service. While it would be a huge gamble, I question whether the company that bent over backwards to provide five-star customer service wouldn't sew up the entire market.

After all, what do you get when you choose a cell phone company? You get a phone: everyone offers phones, and none really keeps an edge on the latest or coolest or even cheapest technology for more than a month or two. You get signal strength and coverage area; those are two big ones, and they make a big difference to most people when they're picking a company, but again, most companies are pretty good in this area, and none is great. You get rates and plans; again, these make a huge difference, but the intense competition in the current market means that all of these companies are pretty close to each other in these areas as well.

So, after technology, coverage, and price, what's left to differentiate? At present, the answer seems to be marketing. Katherine Zeta Jones is pretty and cool, so maybe I'll pick her company (if I can remember which one she shills for). Or that "Can you hear me now?" campaign: it's funny, and memorable. What's that company again? Then again, maybe I'll just go with what's closest to my home. The store nearest me sells for three different companies. I'll see what that guy says I should do.

Or maybe, if my friends keep telling me about the peerless customer service they're getting from their cell phone provider, I'll sign up with that one. My reaction might go something like this: "What, you dial zero and somebody picks up right away to help? ...And they actually *help?!?* You mean, the operator is human? He doesn't merely give you another number to call? Repairs can be done in 24 hours by bringing the phone back to where you bought it? And there's no extra charge for that? Sign me up!"

Such a sea change in the industry might just shake it up. So maybe I was wrong before, when I said these firms have no incentive to compete on customer service. I guess only an actual monopoly, like a utility, has that choice.

Discussion Questions

1.   What do you think would happen to a monopoly if it decided to focus on customer service? Would there be any gain?

2.   Do you agree that if one company in an industry far exceeded its rivals in customer service, that company would steal a significant portion of market share? Why or why not?

3.   Can you think of industries where improved customer service wouldn't help companies to prosper?

Vindication!

While five-star Roche Bros. grows at a respectable, sustainable pace of one new store each year, one of the nation's largest supermarket chains may well put itself up for sale because it has not been performing as well as its competitors. That according to the Associated Press.

The parent company, Albertson's, owns Shaw's supermarkets, which is huge in and around Massachusetts. I can't vouch for the other chains Albertson's owns, but in my area, Shaw's is the polar opposite of Roche Bros.: it caters to the "price first, service and quality last" crowd. In the Shaw's near my home, I've had trouble getting eye contact from cashiers before, no matter how hard I've tried. (I even made my daughter Ayla, not yet two, pay with my credit card. Still, not so much as an anemic smile from any worker in near proximity. The least someone could have done was faked it a little!)

I'm not saying that all Shaw's are this bad – Jane says that, but this is my book. All I know is my own experience. And that experience has me pegging the Shaw's I've been to at one-star, sometimes two.

Intrigued by Albertson's admittedly weak performance, I explored their web site. Here is what I found (synopsized):

Five Strategic Imperatives

1. Cost control
2. Maximize return on investment.
3. Customers first
4. Use cutting edge technology.
5. "Energize" workers.

Hmn. Customers come first? How about third? (Read your own list, guys). Workers come dead last. I'd have to say that someone has his priorities close to backward, and that's what's causing this company to suffer financially. Here's how I'd rewrite the list:

1. Hire the most motivated workers.

2. Inspire them to be proud of their work, their company, and themselves.

3. Teach them customer service values and practices.

That's it! Hire, Inspire; Teach to make your company a H.I.T. My list of strategic imperatives would only have these three things, all about the people we'd employ and the people who ultimately pay all of our paychecks, the customers.

Managers: if you employ the right people, teach them, and let them do their thing, your customers will love you. Your company will grow exponentially. Your stockholders will then love you. And that, as they say, will be that.

Come to think of it, I think I'd add one more item to my list:

4. Stand at the checkout line and watch the profits roll in.

Discussion Questions

1. Do you agree that, in putting its people and customers so far down the list, Albertson's sowed the seeds of its own dismal performance?

2.   What is your company's current list of imperatives? (If you don't actually have one (big mistake!), try to determine what it would be, according to how the company is run).

3.   Do you agree with my list? What would you change?

4.   Are you surprised that customers only come second in my list?

From The Trenches:

Loyalty = Profits

(Where Banks Get It Wrong, Part 1)

Quick question – and I'll bet every reader will get this one right without much thought: What one thing can your bank do to improve its customer service?

Did you answer... "Shorten the lines?" "Open more teller windows?" "Hire more tellers?" Or here's my favorite trend to hate in banking: "Put the greeter to work actually helping people!"

All right, we'll get back to the greeter a little later, because that deserves some attention all its own. Let's start with the lines.

Now, the thing we all have to keep in mind as consumers is, companies are in business to make money, and a key component of making money is *saving* money. In the United States and other industrialized nations, payroll is a company's single biggest expense.

In other parts of this book, I talk about how five-star service in retail involves the customer's basically being treated like a pasha, with personal shoppers, tea served free, and coolies to carry them around in velvet-lined rickshaws for their shopping pleasure. Well, the thing is, all of that is very, very costly. If a company cannot make up this investment with higher volume, then it becomes necessary to set their prices very, very high, becoming what I call Ultra-Retail. And while some people seem to take great pride in paying too much for their purchases, most of us flock to Walmart instead to save an extra buck. Ultra-Retail isn't possible for most businesses.

What most companies do instead is try to follow the Walmart model. They do their best to cut payroll every way they can: employ part-timers for most positions, pay low even though that means they cannot attract or keep talented workers, and provide very few workers to help customers. That's not just in retail, either. Phone trees and automated answering systems are not for callers' convenience. Receptionists cost money.

What companies do when they cut payroll, though, is sacrifice customer service. This works just fine for Walmart. You shop there to save money, and you do, so they thrive. Their business would only suffer if they shelled out more on their employees, because their prices would increase, and you would lose your one reason to shop there. Walmart would begin to face competition.

Now back to banks. If a bank, or any other business for that matter, can slash its payroll sufficiently to provide much, *much* cheaper products or services, it will thrive. Enough people always want to save money that the company in question will be busy and will profit through volume sales. Here's the rub for banks, though: their products are all pretty much the same. Let's face it; the industry has been mature for generations, meaning that competition is fierce. Banks copy each other at every turn. When one bank in a local market offers free checking, the others follow. The big guys have ATMs on every corner (good), but they charge a steep fee when you use another bank's ATM, so you get double-charged (somehow, this is still legal). The little banks don't have as many ATMs, so they don't charge you for using someone else's – but you use other banks' ATMs more often, so you get charged more often by the other bank. Pick your poison. They all get their capital from the same source, so they all pay the same for it. Shop around for interest rates and see what I mean.

That means that there are only two ways for a bank to out-compete its rivals. They can advertise more, and try to build brand recognition and maybe even customer loyalty. We all love a winner, so the biggest often attracts masses of customers, somewhat by default. Think Coke versus Pepsi, and either of these versus RC Cola.

Or, they can provide superior customer service. All other things being equal – price, services/products offered, convenience – we will choose to do business where we are treated better every time.

Again, all banks offer the same products and services. Where they differ – strike that, where they *could* differ, if they'd choose to invest in payroll – is in customer service.

Banking is a zero-sum game. Everyone has a bank. If you come to my bank, that means you're leaving my competitor, so I win and they lose.

Thus, here's the reality: the fastest way to entice customers to switch to my bank, and the best way to keep my current customers, is if I shorten my lines. That means I have to hire more tellers.

Of course, there are dozens more customer service extras to add, like serving the tellers coffee so they're not so damn slow, and making sure they smile from the eyes. It would also be nice if they spoke English pretty well, and if they knew the basics of how their banks actually work, so they can be more helpful. (Can you tell I have issues with the banking industry?) But all of that is icing on the cake. The cake is to put bodies behind windows, so they can shorten lines and actually serve their customers.

Our client, Roche Bros., has a rule in all of its stores: if there are more than two people in a checkout line, they'll open another line. Even if it's just for three minutes!

This costs them a lot of extra money, to make sure they have sufficient staffing. But guess what? Just about every Roche

Bros. store is really busy (read: profitable), and that's with other grocery stores just down the street, and even Walmart with its dirt-cheap grocery department nearby. How do they do it?

People will pay for, and will travel for,
convenience!

And the best way to ensure convenience is to
let customers shop quickly.

- You can't shop quickly if you have to wait twenty minutes in line.
- Likewise, you can't bank quickly if you have to wait in line.
- You can't fix a complaint by phone if you have to wait for an available call-center operator.
- You can't get issues resolved quickly if the person you deal with (in person or on the phone) is not authorized to fix your problem.
- You can't buy someone's product if the sales rep takes three days to return your call.

You see, this section may be about banks in particular, but really it's about all of us. Quick equals convenient equals happy equals loyal. And nothing makes a company more profitable than loyal customers, who stay with you, who refer their friends, and who are happy to be a good reference. (I should know: that is exactly how I have built my business.)

Banks will spend more money if each branch has six tellers rather than two at peak hours. But the one bank that learns this lesson will steal all of its competitors' business, and sooner rather than later.

That is what banks – and most companies – fail to understand. Every time I speak to an executive or business owner who laments that payroll is her biggest expense – and there are a lot of them out there – I shake my head in wonder. Sure, pal, your company made ten million last year. But it could have made eighty million, had you seen payroll and commensurate customer service as an investment rather than an expense. Don't be too impressed with yourself.

Quick = Convenient = Happy = Loyal

(And remember, Loyalty = Profits)

Discussion Questions

1. What can *your* company do to improve the speed at which it serves customers? Would more front-line workers help?

2. Would your company gain a competitive advantage if it acted on this Quick = Convenient = Happy = Loyal formula?

3. Would that competitive advantage translate into more sales? And if so, would those increased sales pay for the added payroll, and thus prove profitable?

4. Think long and hard about question 3. Don't just say, "Of course it would" because you're wrapped up in the spirit of the book you're currently reading. If this plan loses your company money, it's going to fail, and your company's commitment to customer service will falter right along with it.

From The Trenches

"They deserve to be publicly whipped."
- Professor Johnston

As you read the following passage, I ask you to shift your perspective a bit. Since birth, we are taught to revere doctors, and I agree, they deserve our respect. However, the notion that doctors and hospitals are not in business like the rest of us is bizarre to me, especially when you consider the money involved. When you think of the practice of medicine as a business no different from any other, your view on the customer service you receive changes dramatically, I promise you. When you come to see that *patient* is merely another word for *customer*, when you judge the field in terms of customer service, then you will see how drastically in need of reform the entire profession really is.

I had this "colorful" sociology professor in college. He was like Archie Bunker with a Ph.D., but I'll spare you his ludicrous diatribes. Suffice it to say, the most important thing I took from his class was that catchphrase: "Publicly whipped." That sums up my feelings toward the purveyors of one-star customer service more succinctly than anything I've heard.

The first thing I think of when it comes to one-star service is an emergency room. Now, I'm an active guy, and my zest for life brings me into harm's way from time to time. So far, I've broken a bone only once, but I've long since lost track of the number of stitches I've received. And of course, when you're bleeding and have a gaping wound that exposes your kneecap, there's really only one place to go, isn't there?

Now, bleeding says to me, "emergency" or at the very least, "hurry up." A gash requiring a dozen stitches inside and seventeen outside seems worthy of prompt attention. But a few years ago, when a sledding accident landed me in a nearby hospital's emergency room, I had to wait *eleven hours* to see a doctor. And no, nobody on staff was sorry about that in the least. (…And no, no life-threatening emergencies came in to take the staff's energy. It was just another day at work.)

This is what I just can't fathom: the hospital gets paid by our insurance companies. The hospital pays its emergency room doctors. Surely, there's more than a little mark-up there – I *know* there is, because I have friends who were ER doctors just out of their residencies, and they weren't paid all that well. So, if there is always an hours-long wait for service… surely the company (in this case the hospital) can hire another worker (doctor) or three, and move the line along. Its capacity will increase, so it will make more sales (treat more patients).

It's mean to make anguished people wait. I was hungry, bored, wet, and uncomfortable – big deal. But the others with me included some who were much worse off that I. I know I genuinely care about my students; aren't hospital administrators supposed to care about their patients, at least a little bit? And if they do, then surely they can find some doctors to work part-time during peak hours for a little extra pay. Contrary to popular belief, not every doctor is rich, especially the young ones.

It's unnecessary to have endemic delays in emergency rooms, when the demand can keep the staff busy, and can thus pay their wages. And it's abominable customer service. Really, if it weren't so standard in the industry, this is the kind of thing that should get the hospital leadership fired by the board of directors. And that's not bombast so much as plain business sense.

Imagine if you had to wait eleven hours – or even eleven minutes! – at McDonald's. And at McDonald's, you're not exactly bleeding.

9

ON THE TELEPHONE

"There are no shortcuts to anyplace worth going."
- Beverly Sills

To begin our discussion of customer service on the telephone, it probably makes sense to start where your customer does, with your firm's phone-answering system. Let's start with some discussion questions to get us thinking.

Discussion Questions

1. What system does your company employ to take calls from outside? Does a person pick up, or is there an automated greeting followed by a list of options? Do callers have to dial part of their party's name? Are they steered to voice mail if the party is not at his desk? Can they dial zero at any time to get a human? Once they reach an operator, how helpful is that person?

2. Now think about when you call other companies. What features do you like? Which irk you?

3. Companies are adopting all sorts of greetings when they pick up the phone. (For instance, "It's a great day at Second Multinational Conglomerated Bank. This is Betty. Can I interest you in a platinum Visa card with 29% APR?") What greeting does your company employ?

4. Does your company try to encourage a maximum number of rings before someone picks up?

5. What about callbacks? Does your company have a standard time for employees to check their voice mail, or a number of hours (or days) in which to return calls?

6. What happens when customers call after hours?

Of all the aspects of customer service we train, this is the one that I take most to heart. There is nothing that infuriates me more than not getting a human when I call. Label me spoiled or old-fashioned, but when I call a company of any size, I expect a human to speak to me – and I expect them to be knowledgeable, helpful, and cheery. In fact, an ounce of good cheer will cure a pound of frustration. Lukewarm or surly "help" is nothing if not an invitation to take my business and run.

Naturally, this is a matter of personal preference. I have Yankee friends who complain because the operators they talk to are too chatty, friendly, or "fake." Yankees often think any stranger who acts friendly is fake – this does not exclude my mother, who is one of the nicest people you could ever meet. It's just the way we're raised. I don't know what happened to me.

I've also read that a large portion of the calling public actually *prefers* to deal with a machine. I've never met one of these masochists, but apparently, they're out there in droves. (Now that I really think about it, I hope I never *do* meet one!)

Here's a standard that your company, if it is truly dedicated to five-star customer service, would do well to emulate:

Have you ever eaten Domino's pizza? If you have, you're likely to know two things: it's not all that savory, and it's very reliable. (People go out of their way for reliability; just ask McDonald's). And here's Domino's five-star customer service trick: their policy is for a person to answer the phone by the second ring. I worked this job one summer as a college kid, and I can tell you that I never witnessed this rule broken, even on their busiest night. Their shops are often stress factories. But they consistently deliver on their high service standards. (Sorry for the pun).

Many companies would argue that this standard is impossibly high, that employing enough operators for this kind of service would bankrupt them, and maybe they're right. But Domino's makes all of its money through delivery, and their research has shown that every ring increases the likelihood of a hang-up exponentially. Even that second ring adversely affects their bottom line. If they *don't* pick up the phone right away, they know they'll soon be out of business.

I'm a CEO, and I answer the phone all the time. That often surprises people, as does the alacrity with which I pick up. I've even been told by well-meaning friends that it makes me sound desperate, as if I'm sitting by the phone. So be it. As a teacher of five-star customer service, I don't feel I have a choice in the matter.

Discussion Questions

1. How few rings can your company realistically set as its maximum?

1. Is it feasible for the company to man the phones with an actual man (or woman)?

2. Would the benefit be worth the cost?

3. If human receptionists are impossible, at least discuss the level of quality being provided with your current system. Can it be improved upon?

4. What is your greeting? Can you shorten it without impinging upon its quality? Do you even want to?

Smile on the Phone.
It Matters.

If the title of this book could be, "Everything I Know About Customer Service I Learned at the Supermarket," then this section could have its own alternate title: "Everything I Know about Telephone Customer Service I Learned at Lifeline Systems."

For those readers unfamiliar with this company, Lifeline provides elderly and disabled subscribers with a device, worn around the neck or wrist, which they can press if they have an emergency. The button activates a phone in the subscriber's home, which dials the Lifeline call center. Within seconds, an operator is on speakerphone, ready to assist. The operator can then call 911 or a family member, as appropriate, or he can guide the subscriber through resetting the device, if it has been activated inadvertently. This service allows subscribers to live in their homes for years after they might otherwise be relegated to a nursing home. My diabetic Aunt Claire was a subscriber years ago. I can attest from personal experience that the service this company provides is life altering.

Now, even the best firms have to push their own high standards, or their competitors will eventually surpass them.

Lifeline is no exception. The thing is, they *do* constantly push the envelope. And that's why they're the biggest and the best at what they do.

I've spent a bit of time working with the call center operators at Lifeline, and their whole operation is pretty impressive. It's uncanny how caring and nice these people are. They often have to take abuse – after all, their subscribers are old and, when they call in for help, they're usually distressed in some way. You'd be cranky, too, if you'd just fallen in the kitchen and broken a hip!

Cranky or no (and to be fair, most callers are quite pleasant), I've heard nothing but gracious comments from my students, such as, "I love my subscribers. They're so cute, and they need my help."

My subscribers. It takes a special kind of person to work with the infirm elderly, and Lifeline is staffed by nothing but. Operators who aren't caring don't make it through training, usually of their own volition.

The call center is attractive and brightly lit. Every wall is decorated with professional photos of actual subscribers, with kind quotes about how Lifeline has improved their quality of life. You can tell as soon as you walk in the door that even the company's top executives take their mission of helping people very, very much to heart.

Perhaps the most unusual thing I've seen there, though, is the small mirror at many of the workstations. Why are they there? They help remind the operators to smile when they're on the phone.

Can the callers see these smiles? Of course not. Can they *hear* them? Absolutely. If you doubt it, try it out with a friend. Call her with no smile. Then call again, grinning. Ask if she can distinguish the two. Studies show that, even if a smile's forced, your voice will still change when you smile. Your interlocutor will notice, I promise.

Discussion Questions

1. How often do you catch yourself smiling on the phone? What about frowning?

2. How important do you think this little "service trick" really is?

The thing to remember about customer service on the telephone is, the two parties are denied a very important part of communication: visual cues. My field is language training, so if I wanted to put you to sleep, I could quote you all sorts of statistics about which percentages of what go into communication, but instead I'll summarize. When you're on the phone, you can't look the person in the eye or read his body language or facial expressions. Especially for men, it is a struggle to pay attention for long without these stimuli. Then too, the stakes are often higher: your customer can hang up without a second thought; walking away from a face-to-face meeting isn't nearly as impersonal or easy.

That is why your voice, and what you say with it, has to be even more customer-friendly than in person.

The good news is, while the medium is different, the rules of service still apply. There's no need to make up separate standards of conduct for providing five-star customer service on the phone. Simply apply what you already know.

Follow this quick cheat-sheet and you should be way ahead of the curve in providing vastly superior customer service via the telephone.

Five-Star Telephone Cheat-Sheet

1. Apply everything you already know about five-star customer service.

2. Make sure a human picks up the phone at all times.

3. When you're closed, hire an answering service. Alternatively, forward the main office line to the cell phone of a staff member who is "on call" all night or weekend.

4. Pick up on the first or second ring.

5. Keep your greeting extremely brief.

    a. Identify your company.
    b. Identify yourself.
    c. Finish with, "How may/can I help you?"
    d. There is no "d." Anything else will peeve your caller. (To illustrate an acceptable greeting: "Coiné Corporate Training. This is Ted. How may I help you?")

6. Smile from the eyes. (Do you have a mirror?)

7. When your caller asks for a person, by name or job description, say, "Who may I say is calling?" then pass them on to that person, *cheerfully*.

8. If the caller does not ask for someone by name, live by this rule: Whoever answers the phone owns the call. Never pass the problem on to a second party.

9. Don't waste the caller's time. If you can't solve their problem expediently, take their number and call them back.

10. In the case of a complaint, a manager should give a follow-up call to make sure the customer is now satisfied. If appropriate, you can substitute that call

with a *hand-written* letter or an email that is clearly *not* generic.

11. Without step ten, you are not providing five-star customer service.

Note: There's no scrimping here. If you don't follow every one of these guidelines, the best you can hope for is to provide four-star customer service. You'll be lucky if you even hit that, however.

Patience

One last plug for Lifeline: I have never, *ever*, been so astounded as when I first observed one of their operators in action. While I sat beside this lady and listened in on her calls, the same subscriber triggered her unit four or five times – this in a thirty-minute period. Each time, the operator was patient and kind. She handled the call according to procedure, helped the befuddled subscriber reset her unit, and was then on to help the next caller.

After the third call from this same subscriber, I asked if this was common.

"Oh, sure. It happens all the time," she assured me. "A lot of our subscribers are confused. That caller probably keeps bumping her unit when she sits down."

"Doesn't it drive you crazy?"

"No. That's what I'm here for." She was smiling genuinely.

"But, at what point do you cut her off? This can't go on…?"

The operator I was sitting with clearly wasn't agitated in the least by this aspect of her job. "Even if the same subscriber calls thirty times in a night, that's okay. That's part of what they pay for: we're always here. At some point she'll stop bumping her unit, and then she'll stop calling. Maybe her family or a neighbor will help, next time they're over."

Wow. This operator had the patience of the Sphinx. And she was providing five-star customer service. See any connection?

Five-star customer service isn't a job, or even a career. It's a calling.

From The Trenches:

Need Information?
Get it all the first time

This story has a happy ending, so it's hard for me to get all that upset over it. At the time it was happening, though, it wasn't always easy to maintain a serene perspective.

Sparing you pages of gory details, one year not long ago, it took our business nearly five months to get a loan through the bank we'd already been using for years.

It wasn't all the bank's fault; only half.

First, our accountant promised he'd get our taxes done in two weeks. The only problem being, to him "week" meant month. It was a classic example of over-promising and under-delivering, and here's how it happened: every time he requested information of us, he told us – in fact, he swore up and down – that this would be the last piece or two he'd need for the tax puzzle to be complete. A couple of days later, he'd call in search of the *real* last piece of information. This pattern went on and on until finally, one day, he was done. I didn't believe it until the taxes were actually in my hands.

…At which point I drove a copy straight down to the bank. And I eerily began to live the whole experience over again, this time at the direction of the banker.

Please don't misunderstand. These two didn't unearth new aspects of our company's finances that required closer scrutiny. They wanted credit card statements, car insurance and loan particulars, and payroll records. All of which anyone in their roles should ask for the very first day.

I'll edit out the part where our banker goes on vacation and leaves no one behind who is qualified/knowledgeable enough to help me process my application. Or how she does the same thing again two weeks later. Or how the line, "Definitely by next Friday, at the latest" became her weekly mantra. There's no need to even mention all of that.

The part of this experience I'd like to draw your attention to is how both our accountant and our banker seemed to have no pre-knowledge of what documentation they would require in order to do their jobs. You'd think this stuff would be routine for these people. After all, how many taxes and loan forms, respectively, had this CPA and bank vice president processed before ours?

Clearly, neither had a checklist. What's worse, the banker required scads of information that her bank already had (somewhere) from when we got our line of credit the previous year. It should have popped up when she typed in our account number.

Actually, there are so many gems in this experience – especially from the bank – that it deserves its own book. As with the time the banker requested four items I'd just filled out in her office two days before. I went down to the bank, got half-way through filling them out again, when she found the first batch in the middle of the stack that is our file. Not so much as an, "Oops! My bad!" It never crossed her mind to apologize. And she wouldn't have had to if she'd just looked thoroughly before calling me down!

Then there's the line, "You can't rush these things. It'll happen when it happens." She was right: *I* couldn't rush anything. I couldn't anticipate what else my accountant or she would need to finish their paperwork. But *they* should have known, and asked for it all right up front.

Discussion Questions

1. Does this problem sound like anything that has ever happened to you while serving a customer? Have you ever needed information to help the customer, then discovered you needed more details later?

2. Is there a way that standard transactions in your job can be ...um, standardized, so that you always have all pertinent questions ready for your customers?

By the way, just for the record: call me a victim of the Stockholm Syndrome, but I'm actually rather fond of both of these tormentors, especially our accountant. Of course, if they ever get their hands on this book, they won't feel the same way toward me.

10

OVER-PROMISE AND OVER-DELIVER

"Shoot for the Moon. If you miss,
you just might hit the stars."
- Franklin Roosevelt

"Promise the Moon. Give them
the Moon and the stars."
- Ted Coiné

At this point, some of my readers have missed the title of this chapter, because they're so used to the expression, "Under-promise and over-deliver" that their brains didn't even absorb what they actually read. The other half has read it correctly. What they are thinking is most likely, "Huh?"

There's nothing easy about providing five-star customer service. It's fun and exciting, if you have the right attitude. It's a challenge, and it's something to be very, very proud of. But it certainly isn't easy.

Let's take this opportunity to see how each star handles its promises.

No-Star: Under-promise, don't deliver at all.

- For example: "We can't fit your car in for a repair for three weeks. Bring it back then." If you're foolish enough to do so: "I can't give you an estimate. No, I don't know how long it will take." You get your car back after a month, and your car is not fixed. Your bill is $1,200.

One-Star: Over-promise, grossly under-deliver.

- You call a plumber on Thursday to fix your only toilet, and are told he'll be out Saturday. When you call Saturday at five, you get the "Our business hours are…" recording. There is no option of leaving a message. The plumber arrives late on Monday, and does his repair. You are forced to endure his 'plumber's butt.' No apology is forthcoming, no matter how badly you hint. Cost far exceeds estimate. Within a week, the toilet is broken again.

Two-Star: Still over-promising, though under-delivery isn't quite as bad.

- "We're backed up. It'll be an hour at least before you get your pizza." That "at least" part is exactly what you get: your pizza doesn't come for two hours and twenty minutes. Each time you called to check on it, the clerk who answered was surlier than the previous time, and the manager was even worse, saying, "There's no need to call again. You'll get it." The clincher? The pizza has been in the delivery guy's car for most of that time. You ordered extra cheese, paid for it, and didn't even get a normal amount of cheese.

Three-Star: Over-promise, under-deliver.

This is so common, we've been conditioned to not even notice.

- The pharmacy's one-hour prescription filling policy is so much paper: you're told it will take two hours. Same with one-hour photo, but it's twenty-four hours.
- Your brochures are expected back in three days. Instead, it's three weeks. When you look them over, there is a spelling error that was not there when you delivered it to the graphic artist. The good news is you don't have to pay for the second print job. The bad news is, (a) the printer tries to convince you that one little spelling error isn't such a big deal, and (b) even though it's their mistake, it will still take another two weeks for you to get your brochures.

"That's three-star service?" you wonder. Sadly, in my experience at least, this is how business is done most of the time. Three-star is all about 'most of the time.'

Businesspeople simply don't understand the concept behind customer service – that we're all here to impress each other by going the extra mile, and that whoever does wins the most business, and deserves the most pride! The issue of promise versus delivery is the single biggest place where most companies fall short. The few firms that do understand how to do it right are so rare, most people seldom experience this kind of service, and so go through life feeling that over-promising and under-delivering is merely "life."

But it doesn't have to be, and for a select few, it isn't.

Four-Star: Under-promise and over-deliver.

- Promise the lunch will be out within fifteen minutes, bring it out in six.
- Tell your customer (a.k.a. patient) the doctor is running an hour behind, then make sure the doctor actually sees her in forty minutes.
- Estimate the car repair at $600, then charge $450.
- Guarantee your deep-sea fishing customers will catch a fish or the trip is free, then take them to a spot where fishermen routinely catch ten or more fish.

You can do this by happy accident, or you can plan it. A lot of businesses cover their posteriors with excessive estimates of time or cost. Then they deliver sooner or cheaper. In a way it's cheating, to low-ball your customer's expectations like that. Still, a pleasant surprise is always welcome, so please don't think I'm denigrating this practice. If it's all you can do then by all means, go for it – this is a great level of service to reach as your standard!

The previously mentioned practice is so superior to the alternatives, I feel hesitant to even mention something beyond that. After all, most people would be infinitely better off just getting more than they were promised.

But there is one step above under-promising and over-delivering. Pull it off, and no price you set will ever be too high.

Five Star: Over-promise and over-deliver.

- Advertise your clam chowder as the tastiest in Boston, then make sure it is so delectable that you're perennial winner of "Best of Boston" awards; not only that, but your chowder is so irresistible that every president since Reagan has had it at his inauguration ball.

- Offer the most impressive warrantee in the automotive business, then build a car that is sure to last twice as long – then raise your already market-leading warrantee, just because you can.

- Guarantee that all of your flights arrive on time or the fliers get a free ticket voucher, then make sure you never have to give any vouchers. (We can dream, can't we?)

- Guarantee that your language students will improve one level in just 48 hours of classroom time, rather than the 230 hours promised by the gargantuan industry leader. Then challenge yourself and your teachers to see how many students you can get to improve two levels or more in that time. (Thank you for indulging me my shameless plug.)

- Make it your policy to keep your lines to two people maximum – in your store, at your bank, in your insurance brokerage. Then inspire your team to see how often you can avoid lines altogether.

Have you noticed how the words guarantee and warrantee keep popping up in these examples? That isn't an accident. If you believe in yourself, and you want others to, commit to a standard of performance publicly, even legally. Standing behind your work is part-and-parcel of five-star customer service. It speaks to the idea of setting a high standard, and then beating it: what this whole chapter is about.

Also integral to five-star customer service is the self-challenge to push really, really hard – and then to outperform these tremendous standards. Make your performance goals so ambitious that you live in constant fear – no, abject terror – of failure. Let that uneasy feeling spur you to perform even better than you thought you ever could.

If you, as a five-star customer service provider, can barely meet your own expectations, you can be certain that your competitors will not be able to come anywhere close. If for no other reason, let that be your inspiration.

Discussion Questions

1. How can you over-promise and over-deliver in your current position?

2. What practices could your company adopt to institute this across the board?

3. Is it even worth it to try? Or is this standard too high for your purposes?

4. What benefit does a five-star company get from its performance in this realm that a four-star company misses?

The Ethics of Five-Star Customer Service

As my reader may have gathered by now, my work with various companies has exposed me to a wealth of education ranging far beyond teaching the English language to immigrants. One of the most remarkable such experiences I've had came about when I began teaching at Legal Sea Foods' Quality Control Center in South Boston. As my students had significant trouble speaking and understanding English, they were unable to benefit from the company's mandatory two-hour ethics course. This was one of the reasons I was brought in: to teach that course to my students. I joined the next daylong train-the-trainer class. What a remarkable experience!

Yes, you read it right: every Legal Sea Foods employee of any rank, from president to janitor, is required to participate in a two-hour ethics class. Legal is that dedicated to doing the right thing – even though, as president and CEO Roger Berkowitz himself attests, customers aren't going to give two hoots about the chef's ethics if his cooking is bad or the food comes out cold. There is no "angle" in providing this training. I'm not even sure it has ever been covered by a newspaper, which would at least get them some free press.

The program at Legal is the brainchild of two top executives there, Alan Dempsey and David Ticchi, who worked with the Institute for Global Ethics to custom-design a course that best suited Legal's needs. (These entities are remarkable organizations, and I highly recommend you contact them both: the former for a delicious clambake or lobster dinner sent overnight anywhere in the country, the latter to design an ethics course for your company.)

The following passage comes courtesy of Rushworth Kidder, president of the Institute for Global Ethics. It appeared as the editorial in his organization's weekly online newsletter. I think you'll agree that Andersen Windows certainly understands how to over-promise and over-deliver.

Ethics Newsline™ Commentary
July 19, 2004

Windows in the Rain
by Rushworth M. Kidder

Aren't there any good news stories about corporate ethics?

I got thinking about that last week when, to escape a blistering late-afternoon thunderstorm, we tied up our boat at a marina on a nearby island. It was after-hours, and several of the staff were waiting out the downpour on the porch before heading home in their boats. So we joined them. From our vantage, we could see the clouds boiling overhead and the harbor slowly fading behind the rain. When the storm finally hit, we retreated inside -- six adults, a boy, and two dogs -- to watch through the windows.

I've had some fascinating conversations with strangers while waiting out storms, and this was no exception. Maybe it's that a storm overwhelms our petty human wills, forcing us to reschedule the living datebook we call our lives. Maybe it's that our collective vulnerability makes our commonalities seem more obvious, so that it's harder not to need each other. And maybe it's that what sustains the moment is conversation, as engaging and unpredictable -- and yet as purposeful -- as the storm howling outside.

I found myself standing by a window with a man who had spent his life as a homebuilder. With typical Yankee canniness, he found out soon enough what I did for a living. Perhaps because of our location -- with the rain pelting the glass but making no inroads into the room -- we found ourselves talking about the ethics of windows.

He'd been installing them, he told me, for decades. And he'd always gone back to the same company, Andersen Windows -- not only because of the quality of the product and their twenty-year guarantee, but because of their commitment to keeping their word. Again and again, he said, that choice paid off.

He recalled building a house not long ago where, as they sat on sawhorses eating lunch one day, a large windowpane suddenly snapped from top to bottom in a lightning-shaped crack. Over the weekend, two more did the same thing. Turned out, he said, that the company had used a bad lot of glass. Andersen replaced every one of the windows, no questions asked.

He also told me about a house where over time the windows began taking on an odd tint. When the owner called to complain, he phoned the Andersen representative. All the company wanted to know was the measurement of every bad window. A couple of weeks later, he said, a truck rumbled into the driveway. Two men got out in suits and ties, pulled on their coveralls, unloaded their freight, and set about replacing every bad window. As they left, they handed the dumbfounded owner a packet of window-cleaning cloths, a gallon of cleaner, and a long-handled squeegee -- just by way of thanks.

But his most recent experience was the most thought provoking. Back in 1983, he said, he built a summer cottage on an island for a "really nice guy" and his family, and they'd stayed in touch ever since. Last year, the windows began fogging up. My friend wasn't able to get out to check them right away. Meanwhile, the owner got an estimate from another company, which grimly informed him that he'd have to rip out the old frames and redo the beautiful interior pine trim and the well-weathered outside shingles -- all at considerable expense.

So this spring my friend went out to count and measure the windows. He also wrote down the number on every pane of glass. Each number included an "83" -- the year the house was built, and now one year beyond the 20-year warrantee.

"Are you sure that number was 83 and not 84?" asked the representative at the lumber yard when he called them in. "Sometimes the light is funny, and a four can look like a three. Why don't you go look again?"

It was meant as a helpful suggestion. And it could have saved a bundle of money for the owner. But it wasn't right, and the contractor knew it. "No," he said, sighing as he told me, "it was 83."

He didn't hear anything for a while. Then the representative called back. He'd added up the purchases this contractor had made with Andersen over the years. It came to over a million dollars. The replacement windows for the owners' cottage were on their way, free.

Lessons? There must be dozens, but I see four. First, when you let people know you're interested in ethics, you hear great tales. Second, it takes integrity to stay with what's right -- especially when, through a tiny shift in your reporting, you think you could save thousands of dollars for a friend.

So why did the contractor hold his position and not lie about that number? That goes to the third lesson. It's all about corporate America, which (as readers of *Ethics Newsline* know) has been taking a beating over integrity issues. This lesson suggests that when you build a company on quality, service, and ethics, you build loyalties that last far beyond the life of your product. There's another company he could go to, my friend said, selling pretty good windows for less. But he's not budging.

And that's lesson four, which is that what goes around comes around. The company's ethics brought out an ethical response -- even in the face of great temptation. My friend didn't try to put something over on the manufacturer. And in the end he didn't have to. That's a story worth getting rained out to hear.

© Institute for Global Ethics

Used by permission. This commentary originally appeared in *Ethics Newsline*™, a free online weekly published by the Institute for Global Ethics which ended a few years ago.

With this tale, Dr. Kidder shares some outstanding lessons on ethics. Did you notice how good ethics and good customer service dovetail so cleanly? It is quite hard, perhaps impossible, to have one without the other. Dishonest people do not provide consistently good customer service because they're always looking for a way to take advantage. Good customer service providers are honest as a matter of pride, the selfsame pride that inspires them to go the extra mile for the customer.

Discussion Question

1. How many five-star customer service practices can you find in Dr. Kidder's stories about Andersen Windows? Reread the passage, and try to identify at least four different things Andersen did that you have already read about in this book.

From The Trenches:

Spoiled = Loyal

The following five-star tale is taken from my all-time top-ten list of customer service high points. To me, this represents everything that five-star service can be, and it illustrates how even a fairly modest business, charging only a bit more than the customer's alternatives, can uphold the five-star standard on a consistent basis.

My father, though never actually rich, spent his life in a kind of five-star nirvana. Though he was always kind, he still expected (and usually received) five-star service wherever he went. Of course, part of his trick was to live in Westport, Connecticut, a five-star town, and to frequent five-star establishments. Yes, he often paid handsomely for this level of service. But he was happy. To him, paying a little extra was worth every penny.

Self-employed, Dad decided it made sense "for tax reasons" to lease rather than own his cars. I guarantee you, though, that tax considerations did not actually motivate him to do this. Rather, he made the acquaintance of the owner of a small car-leasing firm in our town, and he opted for the service this man could provide.

Dad was never disappointed. Whenever his car needed servicing, the owner would drive to our house, leave his car for

Dad, and drive off in Dad's. The car would come back promptly, always in perfect condition: washed outside and detailed inside. It would smell new inside for a week. The oil and filters were always new, the windshield fluid topped off, as was the gas tank – no matter how low it had been when picked up.

Nor was there a bill to pay. The man worked the service into my Dad's monthly payments, so it was one less thing for Dad to worry about.

Even when he moved from Westport to Boston, Dad kept doing business with the same company. No, the firm's owner no longer picked up Dad's car at his home. But Dad returned frequently to Westport, and sometimes when he did, a phone call would be all he needed to have the car picked up at the friend's house where he was staying, and delivered back there promptly so that Dad could be on his way.

In this way, the leasor won a customer for life (as well as references galore). Because my Dad was so spoiled with the terrific service he received, he wouldn't have been happy taking his business anywhere else.

That's part of the magic of five-star customer service: When you do it right, your customers will be hooked for life. You won't ever have to worry about losing them; instead, they'll worry about losing *you!*

Discussion Questions

1. Try to think of as many ways as possible that this business owner made my father feel special, thus keeping him as a loyal customer.

2. How much do you think it cost the business owner to add the service extras of washing, detailing, changing oil, etc.

3. How much extra would you *be willing* to make in car payments for service like this?

4. How much extra could you *expect to* have to pay for service like this?

5. Is it realistic to expect pick-up/drop-off service, with loaner car, when a car needs servicing?

6. What, if anything, can you take from this example to your own work experience? Are there any inexpensive service extras, like the car wash or oil change, which you could provide your customers?

7. Could your company charge more than it does now, or charge more than the competition, if you gave comparable service extras?

8. If your company did not raise its prices for these extras, do you think it would profit in any other way? Could your company make more money if it offered service extras without raising its prices? If so, how?

11

MAKING THINGS RIGHT

"Difficulties mastered are opportunities won."
- Winston Churchill

If there is one single thing that separates good companies from great, it is how they handle dissatisfied customers. As Joe Curtin of Roche Bros. says, "Follow-through is where you make or break your customer service." When a mistake is made, a four-star company will do effective damage control, and so lessen the ire of its customer. A five-star company will wow the customer, and turn her into its biggest fan.

Looked at in this perspective, it actually behooves a company to make mistakes, just so they can turn contented customers into customers-for-life. Sound improbable? Nuts? We'll see if you've changed your mind by the end of this chapter. (Note: I say that in jest. Please don't start making mistakes because you read in a book that it was a great business strategy).

When I was discussing this part of my book with some of our clients and other customer-service experts, I learned a number of terrific practices that the best firms use for damage control. But it was my own guru, Jane, who had the most compelling insight on this topic.

Jane admitted that Roche Bros. might seem merely four-star to most customers. They're top-notch at customer service, but when things are going right… big deal. How much better than completely satisfied can a customer be? What makes that type of service the best one percent?

It isn't until something goes wrong, Jane noted, that Roche Bros. really has a chance to prove its mettle.

Before we go further, let's back up and observe what each of the stars does when something goes wrong. Here's the situation: your customer is livid. You or someone working with you dropped the ball. A time-sensitive delivery was late, or the wrong thing was sent. The product broke. Someone you work with insulted the customer, or at least that's how the customer perceives it – and keep in mind, the perception of the customer is everything; your opinion doesn't matter in the least. This customer is probably already looking around to replace your firm. Most likely it wasn't your fault, but that doesn't matter. It's up to you to fix this problem.

The No-Star Slap in the Face

I stopped at my favorite donut chain for a pick-me-up on my way to the family cottage on Cape Cod. I asked for "a lot of milk," as always, and the clerk made it too dark. (This happens routinely, and it's nothing to get bothered over). I asked for more milk, but again didn't get enough. I asked for more. The clerk rolled her eyes, groaned, threw my coffee out, and as she was making my replacement, she complained about me to her coworkers, right there in front of me.

When I spoke to the "manager" (read: shift leader, or head co-worker), she didn't see a problem. Now I drive one more block, and patronize a seedier, third-rate chain with much cheerier service.

The One-Star Reaction

Customer: "There's a mouse under that booth."

Staff member (clearly indifferent): "I haven't heard of any mice."

The manager is nowhere to be seen, but the customer is persistent. After a twenty-minute wait, he appears. The customer explains the situation, to which he replies, "Whadda you want me to do about it?"

The Two-Star "Fix"

When you bring up a point of dissatisfaction, the staff member you speak to fixes it. Perhaps that means the still-mooing steak you ordered medium-rare is brought back to the kitchen and cooked a bit longer. Your waitress explains, "politely," that medium-rare means raw. No apology is forthcoming.

The Three-Star Remedy

Option A: You are given a sincere apology. No offer of remuneration is forthcoming.

Option B: You are given token remediation – one free dessert for a party of two – with a half-hearted apology.

With a different type of business, you might get your shipping cost refunded, or an upgrade from coach to business class, or credit for a discount on your next order. Often any freebee you get costs the company nothing, or next to it. Still, it's nice. What's less nice is how rare a sincere apology is, even at this level of service.

The Four-Star Solution

Here's what you do if you want to be truly excellent – but not amazing:

1. Listen.

2. Apologize sincerely.

3. Offer standard remuneration for the customer's inconvenience. This is often generous; a $50 gift certificate (no cash value), or at least free dessert for the entire party.

Remember, four-star customer service is really, really good. If I had written a book about this level of service, you could be sure that it would still raise the bar of service provided by almost every company out there.

The four-star solution is genuine, it's nice, and it puts almost any customer at ease, smoothing ruffled feathers. The listening is done well. The apology is clearly heart-felt. The solution offered is above-and-beyond what most people expect.

But this solution falls just short of knocking anybody's socks off. It leaves the customer with a story for her friends that is negative in all of its particulars, right up until the end, which will be proceeded by, "Well, at least they...." By providing this level of customer service, you haven't inspired loyalty. You've patched the leak in your boat's hull. You haven't replaced the boat.

The first four levels of customer service providers handled their adverse situations defensively, some causing even more upset, the others trying their own versions of "damage control." And the last group, the four-stars, did a good job of it.

Ah, but what does conventional wisdom teach us about the best defense? It's a good offense. Five-star customer service providers turn bad situations to their advantage, and in so doing, they further build their already extraordinary reputations. Here's how.

Building The Five-Star Legend

Follow this formula, and your fortune is made:

1. Listen. Don't forget to wear your sincere, "Sorry, that's horrible" face. And guess what: if you don't truly feel sorry on the inside, you won't appear sincere on the outside. There are no "tricks" allowed in five-star customer service.

2. Say, "I'm sorry" at your first opportunity. (But don't interrupt!)

3. Listen.

4. Listen.

5. Repeat steps 1-4 until the customer is all done.

6. Give them a complete apology, synopsizing what they told you. Using your own words rather than theirs proves that you were paying close attention and that you understand.

7. Listen to the customer's response. (Do you detect a common thread running through this action-plan? The key word starts with an "L" and has six letters). You may have missed something important, and this gives the customer a chance to correct you before you redress the wrong complaint.

8. Apologize again.

9. Usually the customer will be satisfied at this point. Thank her for informing you of a problem that needed to be corrected. At this point, a satisfied customer will go on her way.

10. If the customer is still dissatisfied, ask her what you can do to make it right. Say, "What can I do to make it right?" Seriously. Just like that.

11. Whether or not she suggests it in number 10 (and most won't), offer remuneration of something the customer will value. This does not have to cost your company much, by the way.

12. If she is still dissatisfied after your best efforts, and your superior is not present, say, "I'm sure my manager will want to talk with you. May I have your phone number so she can call you later?"

13. Manager: follow up with a phone call the next day, no matter how satisfied the customer seemed at the end of the exchange. (Note: this has got to be someone with an important-sounding title, or it's a wasted effort.)

Guess what? Miss number 13, and you're still – after all of that – probably only providing four-star customer service. (I say "probably" because the beauty of customer service is ultimately in the eye of the beholder.)

"That's great theory," you say. "How does this formula work in practice?" Here are a few examples, starting close to home, in my favorite grocery store.

My friend Joe Curtin was a store manager before he became his company's director of training. As with all Roche Bros. managers, he ran a tight ship: complaints were rare.

Still, mistakes happen. Common among them is the forgotten bag. If the customer left a bag behind, Joe would run to the parking lot to see if he could find the owner before she drove away. Failing in that, he would check with the cashier to see how the customer paid. If it was by check, he would call the phone number on that check. If not, he would have to wait for the customer to call the store. Once the customer was on the phone, Joe (and every store manager) would follow this plan when the customer called:

1. Listen, then apologize profusely on the phone.

2. Send the wayward bag to the customer's house right away. Not ten minutes later; *right away*. Of course, this means taking a worker out of productivity for a while, perhaps as much as an hour, but so be it.

3. Add something extra to the customer's bag, on the house. Typically, a pint of Ben and Jerry's ice cream or, better yet, a bouquet of flowers.

4. By now it should go without saying, he would call later that day to follow up.

My family experienced five-star customer service following an airline screw-up one time. My sister, Michelle, was on her way from New York to Phoenix late one night, to visit our grandmother, when she was bumped in Dallas. This was the seventies: bumping was common. They gave her the standard airline "fix-it" of a free round-trip ticket within the contiguous US. No room, no meal, no apology, but a free ticket isn't that bad, right?

Wrong. Way wrong. Michelle was fifteen, alone in a strange airport in a strange city, traveling on her own for the first time. It was late at night, and she was scared.

…And was my Dad frosted! Getting "frosted" is how we Coinés show our deepest anger. We don't explode or carry on. We quiet down, calm down, and …boy, you'd never want my Dad to get frosted with you, even if you were the president of American Airlines.

In no time, that's exactly who Dad had on the phone. I still don't know how he did it. Long story short, it was too late to get Michelle on another flight, but the head of the airline made things happen for her, in a hurry. A company driver picked her up at the airport and drove her to a first-class hotel, where she was well fed and put up in a suite. The next morning, room service delivered breakfast to her suite, and then a driver brought her back to the airport, where she waited in the Admiral's Club lounge until just before her flight. She traveled first class to Phoenix and home again; she was even driven to our Grandma's house and back on the airline's dime. A week after the incident, my father received his own Admiral's Club card in the mail, with a hand-written note from the company president.

You could argue that stranding a minor in a strange city was a liability, and I'd agree. Certainly, the airline was protecting itself from litigation. But its response was so outstanding, so over-the-top, that my father – a regular business traveler – became a loyal American Airlines flyer for life. And when his Admiral's Club membership expired after a year, he renewed it thereafter.

American Airlines made a major gaffe, but it recovered superbly. How many times have you been able to reach a Fortune 500 company president at his home late at night? That was the most obvious opportunity for the company to drop the ball, and it didn't. From then on, it was all of the president's doing, and you might not expect less from a person of that rank. But he did it. He made things right. And he followed up expertly.

To reiterate, here's the clincher: before this episode, our family was content with American Airlines, but also with United, Delta, and Pan Am. Afterward, my family flew American exclusively for years, my father for life.

How much did it cost for American Airlines to make things right? A bundle, I'm sure. But how much did American end up profiting off of my family's continued patronage? How much did it profit indirectly, from our endorsement with friends over the past thirty years? And now they're getting plugged in a book as an example of how to do customer service right.

Five-star customer service pays. A lot. It may be an expensive investment up front, but its return is worth many times the pennies spent. And the good news for the few of us who really "get that" is, most people – and thus most companies, including our competitors – will *never* "get it."

Find out what everyone else is doing, and do the opposite. That is one recipe for success I've picked up over my career, and let me tell you, when it comes to customer service, it's law. While every other company competes on price and with slick advertising campaigns, five-star customer service providers can do what they do best – wow their customers – and enjoy the windfall.

From The Trenches:

Damage Control

One day one of our teachers quit, completely out of the blue and only about an hour before her first class of the day. She notified me via email; thankfully, I returned to the office to check it in time to call the manager and cancel her first class. The manager was unhappy, but I apologized so thoroughly and sincerely that she couldn't really be mad at us. I told her I was embarrassed, and it was clear I meant it.

Before I continue, I should explain a few things about how we operate our business. Everything that we do – and I cannot stress that enough: *everything* – we do with our clients' complete satisfaction in mind.

- None of our teachers has ever been late to class, with the exception of me, once. That day I was held up by a blizzard that ended up dumping twenty-eight inches of snow on the state. That day, I was seven minutes late.
- On a handful of occasions we have had to cancel class the day of, but probably not more than once a year on average.
- Likewise, we take great pains not to cancel class for any reason, such as a teacher's vacation, sick day, etc. We strive to send a substitute even if we have only a

few hours' notice. That sub is often me, despite the fancy title of CEO on my business cards – or more appropriately, *because of* that title. Find me a business owner who's afraid of getting his hands dirty, I'll show you a failed business in a very short time.

- We recruit the most dynamic and talented teachers in their fields, then bend over backwards to keep them. Their pay, benefits, and the respect we give them are all much better than they would receive from any other employer. While it makes us proud to treat our colleagues so well, it's only partially about them. Really, it's about maintaining our company's quality of service, which builds our reputation, and which brings us the phenomenal growth we've enjoyed to date. When our students are learning well and are delighted with their teacher, our client is happy, and so are we.

- Keeping the same teacher with a class from beginning to end is a big part of our students' satisfaction. Thus, it is very much in our interest to reduce turnover.

With all of this in mind, it didn't take me more than a few minutes to determine what I had to do. On the one hand, I was trying to write this book, polish our business plan, wrangle a large loan from the bank, attract investors, oversee the development of our online ESL school, find a new location for our headquarters, establish new strategic alliances, polish the details on the patents we were applying for, and guide our new head of sales in his duties. You know, CEO stuff.

On the other hand, a teacher had just abandoned a full load of classes spread among four employers, with a fifth, brand-new client about to start in a week, with this star teacher sold as part of the package. I had just canceled her first class of the day, and had about four hours until her next class started.

I went myself, and I made it my class. These guys were only five meetings away from graduating, and they loved this teacher. I felt the surest bet in this case was to send the company owner. How better to apologize? Plus I'm a control freak, and I knew I could win them over despite their inevitable letdown. While I'm sure that any of my teachers could have done the same, I had to be there myself to see this one through.

I also took her other classes over. And began with the new client as well, even though that was a six-month commitment. It seemed the only appropriate response. My company isn't GM. We're still small enough that I can have a close relationship with all of our clients. This above-and-beyond solution was, in my opinion, the only choice.

Could another of our teachers have taken over and done a great job? Without question. Would that have satisfied our clients? Again, I'm certain it would have. So why did I commit myself to so much extra work, perhaps even to the detriment of some of my other duties?

Because I simply can't run my company from the perspective that excellence is good enough. We as a company had dropped the ball by losing this teacher mid-session in her classes. I gave her students, and our clients, the most sincere and powerful message I could that, while mistakes do happen, how we address them will never be less than with five-star customer service.

Discussion Questions

1. Wasn't it a little over-the-top for me, as CEO, to take over all of these classes myself?

2. In the short-term, my company would suffer from my absence. Was there any payoff you can see in the long run that could justify such a decision?

3. Can you compare this situation to anything that your company might have faced in the past? What did management do in that case? (Remember, the larger the company, the less possible its top leaders can jump in as I did for my small firm. No one's expecting Michael Dell to start fixing computers because one of his technicians quit in the middle of a project.)

4. In the situation you came up with in question 3, how might it have been handled differently to provide better customer service?

As with many of my stories, this one has a footnote worth mentioning. At the time that this teacher quit, I couldn't see much good in the situation. After all, Jane and I lost a friend, and our company lost a great teacher.

Ah, but let things sit long enough and the real boons of temporary disappointment will show themselves.* Sure enough, two benefits came from the classes I took over. One, the Coiné Method, is the culmination of eight years of teaching pronunciation that I might never have perfected were I not actually in the classroom. The other benefit was my friendship with one of her students, an IT manager named Jatin. Long story short, he was so impressed with the results he achieved through the Coiné Method that he offered to help develop the software to take that method global.

*I call this my Lemon Law: no, it's not about returning defective cars. This Lemon Law is the imperative about making lemonade from the lemons life gives you.

12

HOW MUCH DO I
HAVE TO TAKE?

"Do the right thing.
It will gratify some people and astonish the rest."
Mark Twain

Five-star customer service isn't about being a masochist, and letting others walk all over you. There are times (though only a few) when you just have to cut your losses and say good riddance to a customer.

1.   When that customer is abusive.

2.   When it is clear that the customer has no interest in being satisfied, despite heroic efforts on your part.

3.   When that customer's ethics are in question.

The first case is simple: if you are on the phone with someone who raises his voice or swears at you, remain calm and inform him that you are going to hang up because he is not being civil. Give him a chance to simmer down, and if he doesn't, hang up. Even as a five-star customer service professional, you are allowed.

If the person in question is right there in front of you? It might be a bit trickier to extricate yourself in this case, but you have to nevertheless. The trick is to remain calm. Remember, only you can make yourself lose control – and the litmus test of a professional is that she *never* loses her cool. Simply inform the abusive party that you have nothing more to say to him until he shows you some common respect. This may or may not get his attention, so follow it with, "Good day."

Then call security if necessary.

The second case, with the unwilling-to-be-satisfied customer, is a much tougher call to make. When do you give up on a customer? After all, as a matter of pride, this goes against everything you stand for. Do it, and you're going to beat yourself up for days, thinking you could have handled it better. Think of the emergency room doctor who loses a patient, only this should be much, much rarer than that.

Sorry, I can't let you off the hook that easily: usually, you could have done better. Don't give up without a heroic effort at winning the customer over.

But occasionally – and in a truly well-run organization, this is exceedingly rare – you just won't be able to satisfy someone. The time will come when you have to say goodbye.

To quote a friend whose career has been spent providing superlative customer service, "At some point you've got no choice. You're just going to have to say, 'I'm sorry we can't make this right for you. Perhaps you'd be happier taking your business to our competitor.'"

How often does this happen? I asked. "Oh, maybe once a year." He thought for a moment. "No, not even. I'd be surprised if I've said that more than a dozen times. I've been in this field over thirty years now."

Just for those who, like me, are not that fond of math: that's roughly once every three years, on average.

So those are situations one and two in the category of letting your customer go. What about ethical breaches? What's the rule there?

If I were a professor living in an ivory tower, I'd tell you never to do business with individuals or companies that you suspect of being less than morally upright. But you know what? That's usually just not practical. Black and white cases are simple, but morals also have shades of gray - your customer treats you politely, for instance, but is less courteous to his employees. Is that an indication that he is going to cheat you down the road? Maybe he *doesn't* treat you that well, but hey, you need his business. Or maybe he seems normal, but you get a bad vibe nonetheless. What then? You just can't turn down someone's business because they're not nice, or because of silly intuition. So, where do you draw the line?

As I said, the black-and-white cases are a cinch. If you're a lawyer and your client confesses his guilt to you, I'm sorry, drop the case. If the company you consult for dumps toxic waste, I don't care if it means your family will starve, you can't work for them. If you manage a store and you catch a customer shoplifting, your obligation to be courteous has just gone out the window. Call the police.

But we're not talking about the easy ones. Sometimes, firing your customer for ethical reasons has more to do with how much you can take than anything. That's what makes this issue a lot tougher than the first two. I hope these next two examples will help.

Firing Your Customer
Take 1

You may think I'm a freak, but somehow, I can remember the name of every student I've ever taught. That's thousands by now. Maria (name changed for my sake, not hers) is one student I wish I could forget, though.

This Brazilian lady seemed very nice. I'm sure she *is*, to her friends and family. But boy, did she try her best to take advantage of me!

I met her the first month in our new one-room schoolhouse in downtown Stoughton. We had just moved classes out of our living room, and I was still experimenting with all aspects of our business model: how and how much to charge, when to hold classes, how many students to teach at once, how to screen them, what books to use.... Wow, even with years of prior experience, there was a lot to figure out once I was on my own.

I advertised by posting flyers in all of the Brazilian and Russian shops in the town. On those flyers I had written (in all three languages) that there was a monthly fee of $80 for our basic course, which met once weekly for two hours. That comes out to ten dollars an hour – an important point to remember later in this tale.

Maria signed up for her first month and paid, no problem. She came to the first few classes, and then (like many students, as I would learn) she disappeared for a while. When she attended school three weeks later, I asked for her next payment at the end of class – and she was indignant!

This pay-once-a-month model I'd devised didn't work for her. She only took three classes last month, she said, so she had one in the bank.

We went around and around on that point; not an easy feat when neither of you speaks the other's language well at all. Finally I threw up my hands and said, "Fine, pay me next time. The lesson you had today is on the house." She left very happy. Oh, well.

I didn't see Maria for a while, and then one day she came an hour into class. I had two policies about that: first, students were welcome any time. By then I'd long since mastered the challenge of keeping class running without stopping to accommodate latecomers, so I let in anyone anytime, as long as they didn't disrupt class when they arrived.

The other policy was that I didn't accept payment in the middle of class. Students could make their monthly payment before or after, not in the middle. As Maria was late, I decided to catch up with her afterward.

Here's my favorite part. At the end of class, Maria first tried to slink out without paying a thing. When I asked her to wait, she pulled out a ten-dollar bill. Not $80 for the month. Not even $20 for the lesson, which I wouldn't have accepted anyway. She'd been there for an hour, so, at ten dollars an hour, she owed me $10. Right?

If my memory serves me correctly, this is the only student-customer I've ever fired. I refused to take Maria's $10, and also refused to ever let her into my school again.

The point? I hope it's not that I'm mean to poor Brazilian immigrants without two cents to rub together. Rather, what I want you to take from this lesson is that it is sometimes, though exceedingly rarely, necessary to fire your customers. To do so, while not exactly five-star customer service, is a reality that every business must face at one time or another.

Firing Your Customer
Take 2

My firm has only begun to offer contracts quite recently, and then only on request. I am a firm believer that a person's word is her bond, and that the value of a handshake is all that two ethical people need. Our contracts are now available only because some of our larger clients feel more comfortable when everything is in writing. That's just part of their internal tradition.

We haven't needed contracts because we've been blessed by clients that behave ethically. I'd have to say that ethical behavior comes part-and-parcel with the commitment to bettering your workforce. Almost as a rule, it takes an honorably run company to pay for its employees' professional development.

We've been burnt exactly once by this idealism, though. And while it hasn't jaded me, it still upsets me a bit. I suppose, as this is the only case among so many honest transactions, I should just feel lucky. That's what I try to tell myself, anyway.

The company became a client when we hired a teacher who'd been their part-time ESL provider. She had terribly under-charged, so that she simply could not afford to continue working as their teacher: when we snapped her up, she was going to have to drop them to accommodate her new full-time position with us.

However, as they were extremely happy with her, she was attached to her students, and my company wanted this prestigious firm to add to our client list, we negotiated a deal that seemed to work for all involved. She would continue as their teacher, but using the Coiné Method. They would pay us, and we would pay her. Everyone won.

There was one issue, though. She charged this company less than we paid her for her time, even before we began discussing benefits! So, if we kept her prices, my business would in effect be giving charity to this huge multinational company. Or, to put it another way, we would be buying their business.

That didn't sit well with me, so I asked for a meeting with this new client to see what could be done. I met with two managers, who explained that they could not suddenly triple their ESL budget without facing rejection from their corporate office. But all was not lost: we could raise our rates gradually, a little bit each session, until they were in line with the rest of our clients.

That was something I could handle. We agreed, shook hands, and the first class went as planned. We were paid at the rate we'd agreed upon, and though they paid very late, we overlooked it. Everything was fine …as far as I knew.

This company's ESL program was so successful, they asked for even more classes. They also requested a business-writing course for their American managers. We discussed a business-etiquette course as well, to be started the following year.

However, when we sent off their next invoice, which included the incremental price hike and which was marked for payment within ten days… there was no check. Not for four months.

When, after a considerable amount of ducking and weaving on the part of the management, we finally came close to collecting on our bill, the same managers I'd met with earlier denied our agreement. They basically renegotiated our prices, *after* we'd already finished their classes! Their attitude was, "Take the check we're offering or leave it. Do you have a contract?" They were even peeved that we'd brought any of this up – as if *they* were the wronged parties!

That type of situation puts the customer service professional in an extremely awkward position. Our entire ethic has us conditioned to please our clients. When they act angry, as if they are the victims, our reflexes command us to apologize – which in this case would be totally inappropriate. To handle this situation properly, I had to take off my customer service hat and put on my Commander In Chief hat. Defending myself (or my family, friends, or firm) is something I am very comfortable doing; however, this would be the first time I had to defend my company from a client – someone whom you would imagine is on your side.

I wanted to discontinue our relationship immediately, but you can't grow a successful enterprise if you rule by fiat, so I consulted my colleagues in finance, sales, and this teacher. They were pretty split on the topic, but it was our sales manager who had the deciding say in keeping this company on for another round of classes. He said that, as we were still small and our high-profile clients were few, he could really use them in his sales effort. Why not fire them later, when we were bigger and our reputation had grown so much that we no longer needed them?

That's exactly what we did. We taught one more round of classes, we grew, and then we removed them from our client list. Why give such an unethical company the free publicity?

Fortunately, that's the only company we've ever fired. I think such a move took them quite by surprise. They haven't replaced us with another ESL provider: apparently, no one else will work at their prices, either.

This is a business story, but how does all of this fit into a customer service book? Again, it's okay to fire your customers – though only in the most extreme of cases. If a company or individual is unethical, impossible to satisfy, or otherwise detrimental to your business, then by all means, remove them from your Rolodex. Life is too short, your time too precious, to waste trying to turn frogs into princes.

From The Trenches:

Where Banks Get It Wrong
Part 2

(I have to preface this by saying that, for people who have never heard of a greeter in a bank, this practice will sound fantastical or surreal. Alas, it's all too real. Read on at your own risk of horror and indigestion.)

Here's a question: What's a greeter's actual *job*, anyway?

I'm not sure if this is a nation-wide trend, but around Boston, whenever you walk into a branch of my bank, The Mega-Conglomerated Bank and Trust Co., there's a person standing there to ask you if he can help you.

"Sure," I said the first time this happened. ('How cool is that?' I thought, 'I won't even have to go to the window to make a deposit! This guy'll do it for me!') "I'd like to deposit this –"

"Right over there," the greeter said, indicating the line of thirteen customers that began about four feet from us.

I wish I were exaggerating, but I counted, and the number was thirteen. Here were all of these disgruntled customers, and right next to them, there's a buffoon in a polo shirt whose job is basically to mock them – sorry, to mock *us*, as I made customer number fourteen.

As other patrons entered, he showed them where they could find the ATM (right in front of their noses), the seats to wait for the manager (three feet to his left), checking deposit slips (right under his casually resting elbow), savings withdrawal slips… need I go on?

Meanwhile, there were two tellers working (slowly).

Now, this is my follow-up question: If the greeter isn't actually gainfully employed by a job that involves actual …work… then can't he pitch in and man a teller's window when it gets busy?

This is simply the hugest customer service travesty ever hoisted upon the American public. Something must be done!

Oh, and it took me about a year to figure this out, but I now think I have a handle on what inspired this mastermind coup: Walmart has greeters! A top bank executive was shopping at Walmart one day, and said, "You know, the lines here are really, really long, and there's no one in the aisles to help you when you need it. But golly! That greeter at the front when you enter sure makes all that somehow okay. I like this place…." And a job description was born.

Discussion Questions

1. Does your company do anything quite so insidious as having a greeter when what customers really want is help?

2. What can Walmart, and my bank, be thinking? Seriously, someone must have thought this was a good idea. Can you figure it out?

13

THE EXTRA MILES

"First and most obvious,
bring out the three old warhorses of competition
– cost, quality, and *service* – and
drive them to new levels,
making every person in the organization
see them for what they are,
a matter of survival."
Jack Welch, *Winning* (italics added)

Anybody can "go the extra mile" to try to please their customers. A not-so-good Italian chain around Boston serves immense portions to try to satisfy its diners. Many mid-range motels now offer free high-speed Internet access, so that it's almost standard now wherever you stay. Sometimes you'll get a survey mailed to you to tell a company how they're doing, or perhaps your video store offers free popcorn on weekend nights, or your bagel shop has a punch card where your tenth dozen is on the house.

That's all great, and I don't mean to knock this kind of

service – after all, *any* attempt to please customers is a step in the right direction.

But five-star customer service isn't about going an extra mile. There are actually quite a few extra miles to be traveled before you can claim the distinction of being in the top one percent. Here are just a few:

Keep a nice restroom.

> "The condition of a business' restroom is the single biggest sign of its commitment to customer service."
> – Jane Coiné

This one is first for a reason. No customer is going to believe that you value his business if you can't even keep the public restrooms nice. No employee is going to believe her manager values her work if he can't even keep the employee restrooms clean. No boss is going to view you as a five-star professional if you don't clean your own bathroom, just because it needs it.

Discussion Question

1. What star would you give your bathrooms at work? One? Three? Five?

Remember your customers.

George Zimmer, President and CEO of The Men's Wearhouse, doesn't just sell suits. Instead, he sells quality, price, but especially customer service in all of his ads. And why shouldn't he? If my local shop is any indication, his is a five-star organization.

When I met Sarah several years ago, she was the salesclerk who helped me update my eighties wardrobe for the new millennium. Now she's store manager, and I'm not surprised. I may go six months or a year without stopping by, but whenever I do, she recalls my name, my kids' names, and my entire wardrobe, not just by color of suit but also by label! If it didn't make me feel so special and valued as a customer, I'd say her photographic memory kind of freaked me out. But it doesn't; I love it, and I keep coming back for this special treatment, even though at this stage in his business another man might be seduced away by a more "exclusive" (read: expensive) haberdashery.

Sarah remembers me. When I was a bartender, I remembered all of my guests' drinks, even if those guests only came in occasionally. Jane's insurance agent, Renee of Riley Insurance in Boston, knows her and her entire family well, even though she and Jane have only met once, years ago. My fifth-grade teacher, Mrs. Davidson, remembered me by name when I ran across her after I had graduated from college. And I remember how some of my clients like their coffee, which I bring them from time to time.

Weird? Sure. Hard? I used to think so, but now I know better: remembering details about a person isn't hard at all, *if you care*. Our brains are hard-wired to remember what matters to us. Even if you are the type who cannot remember what day it is, as I used to be, when something is important enough, we can retrieve it from memory.

Remember your customers. They'll feel special. They'll come back, and they'll bring their friends.

Discussion Questions

1. Do you remember the name and some personal details of your regular customers?

2. Do your customers realize that?

Toss in a freebee now and then.

How much does good will cost? About two dollars. How much does it bring in return? I'd wager it's quite a bit more than that.

All right, the sum of two dollars was completely arbitrary. But the point I'm getting at is that you can't be cheap if you want to win your customers' loyalty.

Recently, I was at the family house on Cape Cod when I realized I'd forgotten to bring the prescription I was taking. There was no way I wanted to drive back home to get it, but also no way that I could go without it until Monday morning.

I called the local CVS, where Bill Donovan was the pharmacist on duty. He looked up my records and informed me that I didn't have any refills. I explained my situation. I told Bill that I was willing to return home Sunday to take my medicine that night, but I asked if he could give me one dose for Saturday. He said he could, and I drove down to pick it up.

Bill gave me four doses, "Just in case." I got out my wallet, and he waved me off. "It's on me, Boss," he said with a smile. "Have a good weekend."

That's the second free weekend hookup we've had at that CVS; the other was for Jane a few years back. I have no idea the cost of a few pills, but I know CVS has made a substantial return on its goodwill investment. By keeping us happy, they've kept us from wandering to a competitor. As Jane seems to shop there daily for household odds and ends, I'd say Bill's boss owes him a promotion.

Discussion Questions

1. Do you give your customers inexpensive extras from time to time?

2.   Do you bend the rules to do little favors for your
     customers?

Be responsive. Let the customer know you care.

"We Love Our Customers" printed on a pizza box or dry
cleaner's hanger isn't going to impress anyone – at least not
anyone worth impressing. What *do* leave lasting impressions
are acts, including sincere words, which show how well you
are listening and how much you really care.

My Cousins Wendy and Gil recently bought a pool cleaning
business in South Florida, which they renamed Pristine Pools;
my sister Ahndi is helping them run it. The business came
with a respectable number of customers, and the procedures
in place were adequate to satisfy most of these customers most
of the time. …But "adequate" isn't in our family vocabulary.
Wendy, Gil, and Ahndi knew from the first day that they had a
lot of work ahead of them if they were going to transform this
new enterprise into something to be truly proud of.

The company's previous owners were not exactly obsessed
with customer service – which may explain why my cousins
bought it at a bargain price. Previously, when a customer called
to complain because his pool was suddenly green, he might
not reach a person at all – or if he did, the typical response
might be, "Yeah, we'll send somebody out." Followed by a
"click." That service call, when it eventually came, would be

followed by an additional bill, even when the problem was caused by the pool tech.

What my sister or cousins say now is, "Your pool is green? I'm sorry about that. Several of our customers in your area are experiencing the same thing, because it's been raining hard this week, and PH levels are off. I'll call our head tech right now to send him over. If he hasn't called you back in fifteen minutes, please let me know."

With this type of response, the customer (a) gets his problem restated, so he knows he has been understood, (b) gets a sincere apology, (c) receives an explanation to set him at ease, (d) knows his complaint will be remedied by someone of some stature in the company (the *head* technician), (e) knows action will follow quickly, and (f) knows the management is highly interested in the resolution of the complaint.

My sister and cousins are responsive to the needs and concerns of their customers. That is five-star customer service.

Discussion Question

1. How responsive are you to the concerns of your customers?

Trust your customer

Ever go to the store, do your shopping, and then realize at the checkout that you left your wallet at home?

If so, don't feel stupid: it happens all the time. But how does your store handle this situation? At Roche Bros., your cashier will say, "That's fine. Please write your name, address, and phone number on the back of the receipt, which we'll hold onto for you. Then go ahead and take your groceries home. You can pay for them the next time you're here. There's no need to make a return trip today."

How often does a customer rip the store off, going home with her groceries never to return? Most of the managers I asked said something like, "That's never happened to me." A couple said a version of, "Oh, yeah, that happened to me once, nine years ago."

Discussion Questions

1. Do you trust your customers?

2. What would happen if you did?

Warning: There are businesses where this type of service just will not pay. I think a fast-food restaurant or convenience store would go broke overnight if it tried this with its customers who are not regulars. Please, be careful applying five-star rules of conduct to one or two-star businesses.

Remind your customers to pay *before* they're late.

My friend Ron is a bit of a flake. He's a professor, and he makes a respectable wage. He's not too organized when it comes to details, though, and so he's always bouncing checks and paying bills late. Not very admirable, perhaps, but he makes good on his debts, so ...well anyway, that's just Ron.

When he learned I was writing this book, he told me about two recent experiences he had that I should include. Both involved delinquent phone bills, but the way they were handled was completely different: one two-star, the other five.

First, the bad: Ron says he was out of the office one day when he tried to make a call on his cell phone. A message told him that he had to pay his bill before he could use his line again. Ron had to find a pay phone – his cell phone company wouldn't even allow him to use their service to give them money!

About a week later his home phone provider, Verizon, called him to say that he was *about to be* disconnected. The recording said that he could pay immediately by phone, or he could speak into the phone and tell them he would pay online. He chose the latter, paid, and his service went uninterrupted.

People are busy. Even good people like Ron are irresponsible – Ron is literally an absent-minded professor. So instead of punishing your customers for being late, call them and give them a chance to straighten things out *before* they're late. The technology is there to make this process automatic. Use it.

Discussion Question

1. How does your company handle delinquent accounts?

Honor Your Word

When we won our first corporate training contract, I made one gross error: I underbid. Basically, after paying our teacher for class time, prep time, and drive time, my little firm made twenty dollars a week for three months of classes. Worse, my best teacher was tied up four hours twice a week, which meant that she was unavailable to teach more profitable classes during that time. Short-term, this class was more of a distraction than a boon.

Ouch. It took us only a week to realize this mistake, but by then it was too late. I called the client to explain our situation, and she (rightly) said, "I'm sorry, but that's the amount you quoted, so that's what we wrote our grant proposal for, and that's what they gave us. I can't help you." I should have saved myself the call, and the embarrassment.

As company owner, I had two choices: cancel class altogether, or suck it up and learn from the experience. As a customer service professional, though, I didn't have a choice. The show went on, profit or no. When an honorable person gives his word, that word is his bond. If that sentiment sounds tread-worn, give some serious consideration to how often people actually behave this way in present times. If you do, you will stand out as one in a hundred – the percentage of customer service professionals who provide five-star service.

At least we learned a lot, proving my "Lemon Law" yet again. Indeed, everything we did for this first client taught us how best to hold our corporate classes into the future, so we are still benefiting today. And we did the right thing. That, as the saying goes, was priceless.

Discussion Questions

1. What would your company do in a situation such as this? Would you "suck it up," or cancel the account?

2. In general, how important is it that you keep your word?

Note: One of the most prevalent concepts in business is the idea that otherwise honorable people can act dishonorably at work, because that's "the way business is done." Wrong. If you're unethical at work, you're a bad person. And yes, I am very confident with my judgmental use of the word "bad." Morality is not subjective.

Do Windows

I heard the phrase "I do windows" from Krish Dhanam, a colleague of Zig Ziglar's, and I liked it so much that I made it my own.

As officers of our Toastmaster's club, Jane and I are in charge of setting up before meetings, breaking down afterward, and helping out as necessary in between. Ed, Rick, and Jay Roche bag groceries when they're in one of their stores during a rush. Roger Berkowitz of Legal Sea Foods spends hours each week in the kitchen, concocting new recipes himself. John Rockefeller swept the floors of his church. Can you imagine, the wealthiest man in the world picking up a broom and acting as custodian?

If you're a five-star customer service professional, then the answer to that last question was a resounding, "Of course I can!" Being a company president, political figure, celebrity, millionaire, or other person of distinction doesn't mean you're suddenly too good for grunt work; it means that you roll up your sleeves and get dirty without a second thought – because that's probably how you got where you are in the first place, and to change now that you've "made it" is a sure recipe for failure down the road.

Discussion Question

1. Do you happily do windows? If not, I suggest you close this book and reopen it to page one. Your journey to customer service excellence is going to take a bit longer than most.

Do the right thing because you *can* and *should*, not because you must

One day years ago I was writing a novel on my computer when the power suddenly died. Sadly, I was ignorant of autosave at the time, and so I lost about three hours of work. As you can imagine, I was disgruntled.

I looked up from my monitor to see a crew from the electric company working on the transformer outside of my building. As there seemed to be a connection, I went outside to investigate.

"Why didn't you knock on our doors to let us know you'd be cutting our power off?" I asked as calmly as I could.

"We don't do that," replied the crew leader with an indifferent shrug. My letter to the president of the electric company was met with another indifferent shrug, this one in the form of no reply.

"We don't do that." Luckily, I was typing on my computer, not hooked up to an oxygen line, as some elderly and infirm people can be. But life-and-death or no, that's no way to treat your customers. If company policy doesn't demand you take extra measures to provide good service, take it upon yourself. Pride dictates the professional will go the extra miles to best serve his customers.

Discussion Question

1. Right now, think of three things you can do in your work that are absolutely not required, but that you know you should do as a matter of pride.

Hire for attitude, train for skills

Parents, teachers, and coaches can train children to have the right attitude. By the time we're adults, it's usually too late. I won't say always, because I have boundless faith in the human spirit. But to change you have to want to, and there's nothing harder to change than someone else's bad attitude.

Skills? You can teach skills. A person with a good attitude and a modicum of talent can be coached and molded into just about anything in this life. That certainly goes double for customer service. Often, the right people aren't currently providing a high enough level of service simply because they haven't been exposed to it in their lives, and so don't realize a new plateau even exists. My job, in large part, is to open people's eyes to their five-star potential, give them the tools they need to get there, and then get out of their way.

For a ready example of this, think of your average McDonald's. They hire for attitude, train in company practices, and inculcate new staff members in the company's ethic of fast, friendly, reliable service. Infrequently, a manager hires a person with a negative or lax attitude; that person usually doesn't last long, because he doesn't fit in.

Managers: if you don't already, then start today to hire people for their attitude rather than for the quality of their resume.

Your firm's standard of service will improve overnight, even if your new hires make more mistakes at first.

If you want to bring five-star customer service practices to an existing staff, I encourage you to try your hardest: you owe it to your current employees to at least give them a chance. However, you may find resistance or intransigence from some of your existing colleagues. This may sound harsh, but I've got to say it: let them go.

You can lead a horse to water, but you can't make it think. Some people have closed their minds off long ago to concepts such as the Customer Service Ethic. It's not your fault, and you can't help them against their wills. Let them loose, so they can find a company where they better fit in. With hope, it will be your competitor!

If the person in question is a manager? Maybe your *most effective* manager? Excise them from your organization immediately, or I guarantee you, all of your customer service efforts will fail.

If it's *you*, the top manager, who fits this description? Well, then I'm really at a loss for advice. At least you're reading this book; maybe there is hope for you yet. As I said, you have to want to change. If you honestly do want to, then you can make it happen. I suggest you find a leadership coach right away – preferably the most expensive one out there, because we only value what hurts us to pay for.

Discussion Questions

1. Do you currently hire for attitude?

2. Does your present staff suffer from endemically poor attitude?

3. How about your managers?

4. What about you, Mrs. Big Boss? Do you have the right attitude to instill the Customer Service Ethic in your staff, and enjoy the five-star practices that it brings?

Managing for Five-Star Customer Service

The last passage touched on something that deserves its own book: Managing for Five-Star Customer Service. The seminar is currently available through Coiné Corporate Training, and the book is coming soon.

From The Trenches:

The Banker Who Gets It Right

(Alternate title: rich people really *do* have it made!)

Sometimes fate throws you a break. This is one of those stories.

Kelly was the business specialist at my bank when I began frequenting their branch in the town of Sharon. She was new, I was new, I had a check to deposit, she deposited it for me... and she actually had a personality, which was a novelty. We got off to a great start, I'm happy to say.

Kelly's a bit brighter, friendlier, and more helpful than your average worker bee, and someone above her noticed. As her bank grew it also downsized (quelle surprise?), and Kelly was moved to another branch nearby. This was a promotion; because of downsizing, she now had the duties of eight business specialists.

This only lasted a few months before Kelly was promoted again, this time to premier banker. In the banking world, *Premier Banking* is a polite way of saying, *Banking for the Especially Loaded.*

Because of promotions, my banker had been elevated to the world of caviar and yachting. And because she's committed to five-star customer service, Kelly brought me along with her. Deserving or no, I had my own personal banker! What a rush! What POWER! What outstanding customer service on Kelly's part not to cut me loose and stick me with her replacement, my branch's new business specialist.

She gave me the top-secret phone number that actually gets a human when you call. And not only are they human: every time I call, they treat me like the President of The United States. If there's a problem, even due to my error, they apologize and fix it. Sometimes I now make mistakes with my account on purpose, just to hear them apologize for something I've done. It's great.

I haven't paid a penalty once since her move, either. I just call that line, and the charge is gone. And when I walk into her branch and ask for Kelly, everyone kowtows: after all, I must be one of those rich premier banking customers – scratch that, *clients* – if I work with Kelly.

Did I deserve a personal banker when she was promoted? Not exactly, as my average daily balance sometimes dipped below $100,000, the minimum required of her clients (count 'em: five zeros). Okay, there have been times since meeting Kelly when I'd have been happy to have two zeros after the $1 in my account.

But Kelly never treated me like just another schmuck trying to scrape it together to pay one more month of bills, even back when I was one. As she told me, "You may not qualify for a personal banker now, but you will soon. And I've got to cultivate client relationships, so I'm your banker."

In an industry polluted by greeters and by officers who take five months to process a routine loan application, Kelly is one in a million. She's something else, besides: she's the one reason I didn't flee my ultra-colossal bank years ago.

Service with a smile, and a little extra to make the customer feel special. That's what five-star customer service is all about.

From The Trenches:

When Rude Service is Part of the Fun

With all of this talk about service good and bad, please don't be mistaken: there are a few places whose gimmick is to mock and harass customers. Boston has this great bar called Dick's Last Resort, a national chain where the staff is trained to act like, well, jerks! I almost got into an argument with the doorman on my first visit because he told me they don't allow T-shirts. Jane had to take me aside and explain their business model. They accept patrons wearing T-shirts; they just don't accept you if you're thin-skinned.

It's a lot of fun there, especially once you've caught a slight buzz and get into the atmosphere. You stop a cocktail waitress and she says, "Whadda you want?" like she's ready to clubber you. Or you ask for a beer and the bartender says, "No. We're out," even though you can see a full cooler right behind her. When a man orders a light beer, he can expect to get ribbed for being a woman. I tell you this first-hand.

Dick's doesn't give no-star service: people actually line up for the pleasure of being abused there. Overall, I'd say it's probably a three-star joint: nothing special, but they get you your drink and food, so no complaints, either.

And like I said, it's fun – when you know they're doing it as a joke.

That's the difference. When you're dealing with a business engaging in no-star customer service, it's not a joke. As with the pizzeria clerk I mentioned earlier in this book, no-star types really don't like you, and they're not shy about letting you know it.

No matter how essential my own firm's training courses are to the success of our clients, we always consider ourselves fortunate to be invited to help them. Attitude is key to the Customer Service Ethic. If you start losing touch with your beginnings, if you become impressed with yourself and with the excellent job you do, the status your company enjoys, the exclusivity of your product or service; in short, if you come to think of your customers as lucky to have you, you will begin to treat them that way, too. And I guarantee, your business will suffer as a result.

True, there are companies that appear to thrive because they charge outrageous prices and affect a condescending attitude toward their customers. Think of the hoity nightclub with the long line out front, the aloof doormen, the A-list clientele. The crowd of 'beautiful people' will flock to this type of establishment. You know them all too well: pretenders and the nouveaux riche who dwell on abuse because deep down they agree with the sentiment voiced by Groucho Marx, "I

wouldn't belong to any club that would have me as a member."
There are times when snootiness is actually a viable business
model.

However successful these companies are, though, keep these
points in mind: (a) they have no place in a book extolling the
virtues of five-star customer service, (b) the owner may be a
millionaire, her staff well-paid (or not), but she'll never grow
her business beyond a certain and, I would argue, petty level,
and (c) take note of how many of these businesses enjoy only
flash-in-the-pan success. I used to live in mega-trendy South
Beach, where the hottest clubs and restaurants are lucky to
be "in" for part of a season. Arrogance is no way to build a
successful, long-term business.

If you still can't swallow this, think of a different
style of five-star company: the private bank. For a few
hundred years now, ultra-rich bankers have been giving
unimaginably excellent service to their ultra-rich peers.
These clients bank by appointment only. They come and
go through unmarked and well-guarded doors. Inside, they
are served tea in fine china, sit in sumptuously appointed
offices, and are kowtowed to by the crème of the financial
world's crème. Billions of dollars are moved each day in
this personalized setting. At no time is the service snooty
in the least.

Discussion Questions

1. Before reading this, did you look upon snooty and abusive service with envy, thinking something like, "I wish I were important enough to go to places like that!" Do you still feel that way?

2. Is it clear by now that even the fanciest establishments out there can and do provide superlative service without copping an attitude?

Take The "Star" Quiz

How would you rate these examples of customer service? Please assign each a star. If necessary, return to Chapter II for a quick review.

1. When you call, a human picks up. All you need is to say your name, and your account information pops up.

2. A gourmet ice cream shop weighs its servings. You are charged 50 cents extra for jimmies (chocolate sprinkles).

3. This is very common: restaurants that charge an extra $1 for blue cheese dressing, or for Caesar salad rather than the house salad that comes with an entrée.

4. Self-serve gas.

5. You call a company and are asked by the automated system to enter your account number. You do as you are told, and then reach a human operator. He asks you for your account number.

6. You call the electric company about your bill, and are forced to listen to a recording about a power outage in another part of the state before your options are listed.

7. The bad news: you're on time for your reservation, but your table is still occupied. The good news: the manager takes you to the bar, where your first round of drinks and an appetizer are on the house.

8. You reach an automated phone system, which lists your options. The only problem is, none of them are what you need. You press zero, and hear, "Exiting system. Goodbye."

9. You reach an automated phone system and are told you have to wait. The expected wait time is _____ minutes.

10. Any bank, anywhere. (Unless you have a private banker.)

11. Your doctor works nights and weekends, because that's when you don't.

12. Parking is not available/ lot is full early. A long walk is required.

13. Required valet parking.

14. Optional valet parking.

15. Optional valet parking at no charge.

16. The bartenders pour every drink with a shot glass, or they use an automatic measuring system.

17. Parking fee is reduced with doctor/store validation.

18. A diagnosis of "cancer" is treated like an emergency. With a call from your internist, the oncologist can see you the same day.

19. You suddenly realize late in the day on Friday that your prescription will run out before the weekend is over. You call your doctor for a call-in refill, but the office is closed

20. You call your bank's customer service line, and the recording says, "Pay close attention as your options have changed." However, the options haven't changed in 18 months.

Now What?

By now, you've read scores of anecdotes illustrating dozens of lessons about customer service, showing you both what *to* do and what *not to* do. As the motto of Coiné Corporate Training reads, *Knowledge Is Power*. But that's actually only half of the story. Knowledge alone isn't anything if you don't use it. *Applied* knowledge is power.

With hope, you haven't made it to the end of this book without modifying the customer service you provide (I hope for the better). Unless you're dead or really, really set in your ways, the things you've been reading began to settle in from the very first pages, and you began to apply some of the lessons in your daily routine from that time. (Note: If you suspect you're dead, seek medical attention).

So what did you learn? Even with all of the tales, and all of the fine points I try to bring out with them, all I ever really intended you to learn can be summed up in one short phrase: The Customer Service Ethic.

Five-star customer service isn't about tricks or shortcuts. It's about values. The best in the field of customer service – and by now I hope you agree, we are all deeply immersed in that field – conduct themselves according to a single principle, just as George Boldt did a century ago: Pride.

If a renewed sense of pride is all you get out of this book, I've done my job. If that pride affects your work, your behavior, your attitude; if it permeates everything you do, then you're doing your job.

You're not guaranteed to be a five-star customer service professional by now. A lot of that depends on where you started, on how dedicated you are to the ethic you've learned, and a bit, just a bit, on what natural talents you bring to the game (although I choose to believe that talent can be learned, and is not merely the luck of our genetic draw).

But I will promise you this: all you have to do is start, and you're already halfway there. Most people either don't know where to start, or don't care enough to bother. …And that's if they're even aware that they could improve in the first place.

You've read this book: clearly, you care. If you paid attention, it should be easy to improve. So keep at it. Practice all day, every day. Evaluate yourself based on the reaction you get from those you serve – and remember, no matter what your position, customer service is all about serving others.

And don't stop learning. This book shouldn't be the end of your customer-service education; it should be the beginning!

Buy more books, and tapes for your car. Go to seminars. Put yourself in situations where you can observe five-star customer service in action, even if that means spending a little extra for lunch sometimes. Chalk it up to research. (How much did your college education cost you?) Evaluate for yourself: is this good customer service? Excellent? Extraordinary? What would you do in this situation to improve the service you're getting, or witnessing? How can you apply that knowledge to your own work, and your own life in general?

For the moment, you've read enough. It's time to Do! Go out into the world, fledgling five-star customer service professional, and Shine!

Printed in the United States
by Baker & Taylor Publisher Services